THE STORY OF MONEY FROM THE STONE AGE TO THE INTERNET AGE

ROBERT D. LEONARD JR.

FULLY ILLUSTRATED, INCLUDING MANY IMAGES
FROM THE COLLECTION OF CHARLES J. OPITZ

FOREWORD BY
KENNETH BRESSETT

Whitman
Publishing, LLC
PUBLISHING SINCE 1934
www.whitmanbooks.com

CURIOUS CURRENCY

THE STORY OF MONEY FROM THE STONE AGE TO THE INTERNET AGE

www.whitman**books**.com

ISBN: 0794822894
Printed in China

If you enjoy *Curious Currency*, you will also enjoy *Milestone Coins: A Pageant of the World's Most Significant and Popular Money* (Bressett), *America's Money, America's Story* (Doty), and *Coins: Questions & Answers* (Mishler), each of which explores the odd and curious things people have used as money.

For a complete catalog of numismatic reference books, supplies, and storage products, visit Whitman Publishing online at www.whitman**books**.com.

CONTENTS

ABOUT THE AUTHOR

Robert D. Leonard Jr., a collector of odd and curious money for more than 50 years, is a Fellow of the American Numismatic Society and the Royal Numismatic Society. He has been a member of the American Numismatic Association since 1961, and a member of the International Primitive Money Society since 1989.

He is the author of two dozen studies of specific unusual monies, plus a survey of the field for *Coin World*. His work has been honored by the American Numismatic Association with three Heath Literary Awards, as well as by three awards from the Numismatic Literary Guild. He was lead author for the second edition of *California Pioneer Fractional Gold by Walter Breen and Ronald J. Gillio*, published by Bowers and Merena Galleries in 2003.

ACKNOWLEDGMENTS

Thanks to all who supplied illustrations (see Photo Credits, pp. 144–146), and to Charles J. Opitz, Q. David Bowers, Carl Wolf, and Janet Leonard, who read portions of the text and offered comments.

FOREWORD

The use of money today is so ubiquitous that we seldom give thought to why it functions the way it does, how it came to be, or what we would do without it. People are paid for the work they do, or for their creative efforts or skills, and they spend that recompense for things they desire that have been provided to them by others. The bridge between effort, compensation, and reward is what is known as "money." It is the necessary medium that keeps commerce functioning in an orderly manner without constantly negotiating the value of services verses products or payments.

It often comes as a surprise when people learn that trade items, coins, and diverse forms of money have been used for thousands of years. An even greater revelation is that barter and trade must have played a crucial part in the early beginnings of civilized contact between prehistoric clans.

The desire to exchange surplus items for different things that were needed was the driving force in establishing customs and rules about how various items should be valued and how interchanges should be carried out. The ultimate solutions became what are now inclusively known as "money." The long road to the variety of monies used today was not a straight path. Hundreds of different items have been used to accommodate the diverse needs of everyday commerce and trade by different societies throughout the years. Some of the items that were used defy credulity. Others have stood the test of time.

In its most succinct form, "money" can be anything that is acceptable to both parties in facilitating an exchange of goods or services between them. In actual use, anything and just about everything has been used as this bridge. Over the years most societies have agreed that precious metals—mainly gold, silver, and copper—are the most convenient and widely acceptable storehouses of value and thus the ideal medium of exchange for all goods and services. Even these, however, have their shortcomings. There simply is not a sufficient supply of these precious metals to serve the economic needs of the world.

Throughout the years specialized needs of various societies have been met by sanctioning unique forms of exchange. Some of these defy logic by today's standards, but are probably no more implausible than our use of electronic transfers or plastic credit cards would seem to people even one hundred years ago. The scope and variety of strange monies of the past is further complicated by a general misunderstanding of the use of these objects as trade items, ornaments of personal wealth or status, barter goods, coins, tokens, and promissory payments.

In this book's fresh approach to understanding the nature of money in all its various forms, author and researcher Robert Leonard presents an entertaining overview of what can only be called a most unusual and bizarre assemblage of items that were once used to facilitate trade. While it is difficult to comprehend how stones could ever be used as money, they most certainly were and their story is told at length by this author. Stone money is only one of the many unusual items described and shown in this composition.

The story of money, in a very real sense, is the story of world history. Not in the stuffy schoolbook sense, but when stories about money are tied to world events they speak of actual actions. Money, in the form of coins, contracts, odd objects made of shells, beads, cloth, or stone were part of the wars, famines, growth, and glory days of many nations. A study of what has served as money, past and present, can help everyone better understand its nature and use through prosperous and troubled times and how it functions today.

When some Neolithic man fashioned the first useful stone or flint tools they must have quickly become coveted trade items that could be exchanged for the surplus food gathered by other clansmen. Little could these early people realize that this convention was to be the beginning of commercial transactions that would impact the entire world and nearly every facet of life thereafter. Such primitive exchanges were scarcely much different than the bartering that went on in America when the Forty Niners left their homes and traveled to California in search of a golden dust that they could trade for whatever luxuries they wanted.

Only a few hundred years ago, in the days when America was still a British colony, tobacco, lumber, furs, musket balls, and beads took the place of sparse silver and gold coins. At that time barter with farm products, known as "country pay," served our ancestors well for many years. It is, in fact, still used to some extent today in rural communities.

Knowledge of how the various forms of money served economic needs in the past may hold clues as to how money should be regarded today, and how people can cope with the universal concerns about inflation, credit problems, management of wealth, and governance. Mr. Leonard's provocative study of how hundreds of societies have adapted to using nonstandard items to meet their needs can only lead to the conclusion that most forms of money and wealth are based on faith, and in the end may all be ephemeral.

What many term as "odd and curious," "primitive," "strange," or "traditional" money, is really not so bizarre after all. It was only through a combination of chance and necessity, that at some time and place some societies preferred to use feathers or stones rather than to rely on electronic blips or pieces of paper.

Kenneth Bressett
Colorado Springs, Colorado

WHAT IS MONEY?

Whatat is money? We use it every day without giving it a thought. But money isn't limited to coins and currency; it includes a wide range of so-called "primitive" (or "traditional") money, surrogates for money, and even things that are quite invisible.

There is no consensus among economists as to the proper definition of money. Many have resorted to a listing of its functions, including some combination of: (1) a legal tender, (2) a means of payment, (3) a medium of exchange, (4) a measure or standard of value, (5) a unit of account, (6) a standard of deferred payment, and (7) a store of value or wealth. Certainly several of these overlap to some degree, and some lists have only three or four of them.

"A legal tender" means that it is required to be accepted by creditors at its lawful value, independently of any intrinsic value it might possess. "A means of payment" is clearly essential. "A medium of exchange" means that money can pass from hand to hand to buy things, though this may not differentiate it from articles preferred for barter. "A measure or standard of value" signifies that it is a scale to compare the worth of dissimilar items fairly, and not just a favorite trade item. "A unit of account" indicates that records are kept by this money standard, though other currencies or goods may in fact be tendered (and the unit of account itself may be entirely hypothetical or a "ghost coin," no longer minted). "A standard of deferred payment" relates to the belief that it will have a stable value in the future. And "a store of value or wealth" shows user confidence that the money has a reasonable degree of permanence.

But it is "means of payment" that is paramount. British Museum numismatic curator Joe Cribb defined money as "any object (or record of that object) which is regularly used to make payments according to a law which guarantees its value and ensures its acceptability."[1] While this is a good start, Alan Greenspan, former chairman of the Federal Reserve Board, added a new element in his remarks at the opening of an American Numismatic Society exhibition, The History of Money, at the Federal Reserve Bank of New York, January 16, 2002: "To accept money in exchange for goods and services requires a *trust* [emphasis added] that the money will be accepted by another purveyor of goods and services. In earlier generations that trust adhered to the intrinsic value of gold, silver, or any other commodity that had general acceptability."[2]

In simplest terms, then, money is "anything used to make a payment that the recipient trusts can be reused to make another payment." This includes items used as money only for special purposes or situations, such as bride-price, funeral offerings, *heiliges geld* (offerings made to propitiate deities), trading with Westerners, or usage only by native chiefs. Among these, bride-price is payment made to the bride's parents as compensation for their loss of her valuable work services. Economist Bernard Laum proposed the term "heiliges geld" to describe objects donated to Greek temples, such as iron spits *(obelos)*, but such special-purpose (originally) money is also found in other cultures.[3]

"Primitive money," however, is often less primitive than we suppose, and frequently holds its value better than our "modern" paper money. After World War II, the United States took over the administration of the Caroline Islands from Japan, who had been preceded by Germany and Spain. Informed of the proposed substitution of U.S. dollars for Japanese yen, a Yapese chief remarked, "First Spanish money no good, then German money no good, now Japanese money no good. Yap money always good!"[4]

This stability was accomplished by restricting supply. The anthropologist William Davenport wrote, "Lacking the power to regulate demand (by such devices as manipulation of the interest rate), primitive societies must rely on measures that control the supply of currency against the demand in their completely free markets. Frequently the supply is limited by natural or social circumstances beyond the control of its users, much as the scarcity of gold or silver once set the value of the dollar or the pound. Often, however, the nature of the currency is such that the society could 'mint' it without limit. Scarcity is then maintained by some convention that, through consumption, destruction or deterioration, renders the currency valueless and withdraws it from circulation."[5] In some cases limitation of supply was achieved by restricting production to certain areas or certain ritually acceptable makers, or by banning production altogether and making do with heirlooms.

This book explores the development of money from the Stone Age to the Internet Age, presenting an overview of the field of "primitive" and other unusual money under the broad categories of raw materials, useful articles, ornaments, customary objects, and money substitutes, with emphasis on actual usage. These distinctions are necessarily somewhat arbitrary, as useful articles used as money are frequently transformed into mere customary objects, such as axes too small or too flimsy to chop with, knives too fragile to cut with, or shirts too small to wear. Likewise, precious metals, though covered under raw materials, are frequently ex-ornaments that have been converted into raw material money. The examples of money given here are for the most part highly selective, and—particularly for customary objects—far more could be supplied. But the study of these odd and curious monies has lessons for our economy today.

RAW MATERIALS

From early times, essential and desirable raw materials—hard stones and metals—were items of barter. When exchanged as objects of uniform size, or by weight, they became more than a medium of exchange, but a measure of value as well. Their permanence made them a store of value and probably a standard of deferred payment as well. Thus they morphed into a proto-money, though generally without the legal authority which Aristotle held to be essential for true money.[1]

Flint

Stones were first worked into tools by early hominids more than two million years ago, with flint the most favored material because of its ease in chipping, hardness, and sharp cutting edge.[2] Exchanges of flint for other articles must have occurred in Paleolithic times.

Flint roughout (actual size)

It was not until the Neolithic Age, however, that clear evidence of organized trade appears. In Britain circa 4000 to 2000 BC, flint was mined on a large scale at Grime's Graves and Harrow Hill using red deer antlers as picks and the shoulder blades of oxen as shovels.[3] Flint from these mines was shaped into "roughouts" for axes, to be finished and polished by the end user. These roughouts range in length from about 4 to 7-1/2 inches, and are found at considerable distances from the mines. They were certainly used in trade by the flint miners, and if sufficiently uniform may have had a definite value as well.[4]

Hopewell stone disks

In pre-Columbian America, the Hopewell culture flourished in southern Ohio and adjacent areas from circa 100 BC to AD 400. They built huge mounds, up to 30 feet high—the largest of which contained more than 250 graves—and some chiefs had their own multi-acre burial mounds. Stupendous quantities of grave goods were interred: one Ohio mound contained more than 7,000 roughly chipped flint disks.[5]

A Hopewell cache in Illinois, not in a mound, consisted of 39 "expertly chipped" spear blades about 4 inches long by 3 inches wide, plus scrapers, eight unfinished blades, eight spear blade roughouts, and four irregular cores. In 1951, University of Illinois Professor John C. McGregor concluded that these points were too finely made to be used for hunting or war, and far beyond the needs of one man, so they "undoubtedly represent[ed] the wealth of an individual."[6] While some of these so-called "cache blades" are finely finished, others resemble rough-outs for spear points. The Hopewell people traded for flint from as far away as South Dakota.

Other Native American cultures hoarded cache blades also. Eight rough flint blades, 4 inches by 3 inches and smaller, were found in 1974 near Palestine, Illinois. They are thought to have belonged to the Albee Complex of the Late Woodland culture (circa AD 500 to 1000).[7] Similar blades were also produced in the Midwest up until European contact.

Obsidian

Obsidian is a natural volcanic glass, typically jet black. It is actually harder than ordinary window glass and produces razor-sharp edges when it fractures. Because of its hardness and sharpness, obsidian was favored for the manufacture of blades and points during the Stone Age.

Since obsidian is found in only a few areas, it was traded over distances as long as 1,750 miles, sometimes as finished tools but later as raw material. In the ancient

Near East, there were two major sources, both in Anatolia. Obsidian from these sources is found over a wide area, from eastern Anatolia to southern Mesopotamia— up to 775 miles away. By about 7500 BC, a long-distance trade net

work was in place, with obsidian the major item traded, primarily in the form of cores and blanks.[8] One city in Anatolia, Çatalhöyük, became wealthy from a well-organized trade in obsidian around 6500 BC.[9]

Anatolian obsidian
(actual size)

Obsidian use generally decreased with distance from the source during the period from 7500 until 5500 BC. At that point whole villages began to specialize in particular raw materials or crafts. The final phase occurred about 5000 BC, with the appearance of the first wholesalers. The former pattern of regular decline in usage as distance increases from the source of supply was broken, with occasional *increases* at distant locations that are thought to have been wholesale centers.[10]

Other ancient sources of obsidian were in Greece, Sicily, and Sardinia. About 3000 BC, obsidian from Lipari in the Aeolian Islands, off the northern coast of Sicily, was shipped as far west as Spain, about 800 miles away, and as far east as Pergamum, more than 650 miles distant.[11]

Obsidian was also traded over long distances in Mesoamerica, another area with abundant supplies, perhaps as early as 6500 BC. The most important sources were in the Valley of Mexico, northeast of Tenochtitlan. Around 1000 BC, obsidian from here was traded as far as Guatemala, more than 675 miles away. In Guatemala itself, obsidian from other sites was exported up to 125 miles away beginning about 1800 BC, in the form of large flakes, large flake fragments, and chunks.

Mexican obsidian
(actual size)

Circa 500 to circa 200 BC, chiefs apparently began to control most of the Mesoamerican obsidian trade: resources were pooled and limited workshop production began at major regional centers. After 200 BC state involvement increased; the city of Teotihuacan dominated many aspects of distribution, procurement, and manufacturing. Eventually, at least 12 percent of the total population was devoted to obsidian working, and about 60 percent manufactured implements for long-distance exchange. In fact, obsidian profits may have paid for the famous Pyramid of the Sun. Throughout this period the principal export of the Valley of Mexico was obsidian, normally exchanged for maize.[12]

In 19th- and 20th-century Papua New Guinea, obsidian from the Williamez Peninsula was traded by boat in the form of cube-shaped pieces the size of coconuts. In northeastern New Britain itself, one such chunk was worth only a single clay pot. But when transported 250 miles west to Sio, it would buy a dozen pots or more. Another obsidian source was in the d'Entrecasteaux Islands, east of Papua. Obsidian pieces were also used in trade there, valued at one plaited fiber belt each.[13]

Silver

Beginning about 2400 BC, Mesopotamian cuneiform tablets mention silver being weighed out to official standards for rents, taxes, and compensation for injuries. By the Third Dynasty of Ur (2112–2004 BC), many merchants were keeping "silver-balanced" accounts, in which they recorded an equivalent value in silver for each of the many commodities they began with as capital and that they expended, and calculated the remainder as an amount of silver also, so that the account balanced. Silver was thus used as money, in the sense of a standard of value, even if most transactions were direct barter.[14]

Ancient precoinage silver hoard

Silver use spread to the population at large fairly quickly; for example, the Code of Hammurabi, circa 1700 BC, set the fee of a physician at 10 shekels of silver for healing a man, five shekels for a peasant, and two shekels for a slave.[15] Abraham—who according to Genesis came originally from Ur (circa 1850 BC, per *Jerusalem Bible* chronology)—purchased the cave of Machpelah in Hebron as a burial place for his wife Sarah from Ephron the Hittite for 400 shekels of silver, according to the weights current among the merchants (Gen. 23:16).

No examples this early are known, but there are finds of pre-coinage silver from circa 1400 to 400 BC from the Persian Gulf, Mesopotamia, Anatolia, Syria, Israel, Egypt, and Cyprus, and the weighing out of silver is mentioned in one of the laws of Solon of Athens. While rough ingots (of all sizes and totally irregular in appearance) are common in hoards, most consist largely of what is termed *hacksilver*; that is, chopped pieces of small, smooth ingots, usually rectangular or finger-shaped, with an occasional intact bar or round ingot.[16]

A majority of hoards include cut jewelry. In nearly every case, earrings—whole and cut—are present, as well as bracelets and plaques. Wire, sheet silver (folded), chains, and an intact ewer have also been found in these hoards. Even chopped-up Greek coins of the fifth century BC have turned up in a find from Egypt.[17]

Viking silver hoard (25% actual size)

Uncoined silver reemerged as money under the Vikings. From about AD 850 to 950, more than 700 hoards of hacksilver, together with more than half a million Islamic, Frankish, Byzantine, and Anglo-Saxon coins (some cut in pieces), were buried by Vikings in Gotland, Sweden, alone. Similar hoards have been recovered in Denmark, Germany, the Netherlands, Russia, and the United Kingdom.[18] About 40 kilograms of silver in the form of hacksilver, plus 8,600 mainly English coins, were found in the Cuerdale hoard in Lancashire, England.[19]

The name of the Russian ruble, originally a silver ingot such as those found in Viking hoards, comes from the White Russian verb *rublit*, "to cut" or "to cut off."[20] They may have been preceded in Lithuania by boat-shaped silver ingots called *grivna* or *kapa*.

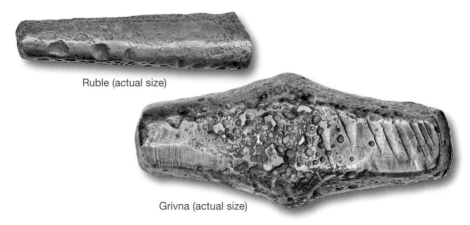

Ruble (actual size)

Grivna (actual size)

Sycee and Other Chinese Silver Ingots

Silver ingots were used as currency in China prior to 221 BC. At first, a variety of fixed shapes were made: cake (called *bing* up to AD 581), rectangular tablet (*hu*), flat (*ting*), and bar (also called *ting*). Later, ingots were cast in the shape of Chinese shoes and renamed *yuan bao*.[21] Such ingots dominated trade until 1933, when they were prohibited.

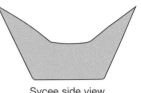

Sycee side view

These ingots were called *hsi-ssu* in Cantonese—in English, sycee ("fine silk," meaning pure, because of the fine, threadlike circles found on high purity ingots, caused by tapping the mold as the silver

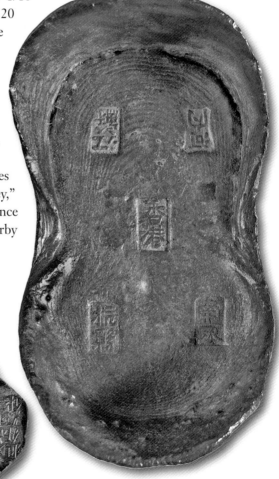

cooled). Sizes ranged from tiny 1/10 tael up to monster 100-tael (120 troy ounce) ingots, though the most common weights were one, five, 10, and 50 taels. Modern sycee ingots were marked with the maker's name, place, and date of manufacture, often with the weight, fineness, and other information as well.[22]

Other Chinese ingot shapes include so-called "saddle-money," made primarily in Yunnan Province after 1875 for export to nearby Burma and Siam.[23]

Saddle money
(actual size)

Sycee silver
(actual size)

Copper and Bronze

Around 5500 BC, copper began to be exploited in Asia Minor and Mesopotamia, ushering in what is called the Chalcolithic Age. With the addition of tin, it was converted to the harder bronze, bringing in the Bronze Age, which lasted as late as 1000 BC. Copper and bronze tools were superior to most stone tools; copper thus became a highly desired trade item, essential all over the ancient world.[24]

As early as the Middle Kingdom of Egypt (circa 2000 BC), slaves were rented in exchange for copper. More than 500 years later, during the New Kingdom, the rental fee for draft animals was also estimated in copper. At this time copper had only 1/100th the value of silver, though two *deben* (182 grams) of copper would purchase about two bushels of wheat.[25] Copper developed into a standard of value, and to some degree a medium of exchange in the form of copper rings.[26]

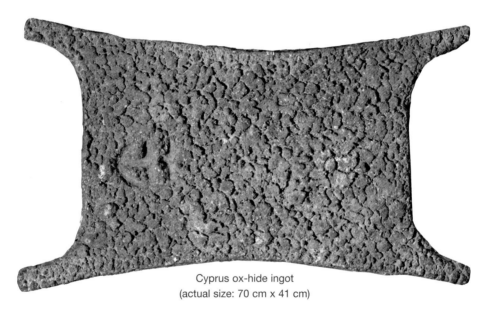

Cyprus ox-hide ingot
(actual size: 70 cm x 41 cm)

Cyprus became so famous for its copper mines that its name in Greek, *Kypros*, means copper. Around 1400 to 1150 BC, Cypriot copper was traded throughout the Mediterranean in the form of thick ingots cast in the shape of a rectangle with concave sides, resembling an ox hide. The corners were drawn out into handles for ease in carrying.[27] Ox-hide ingots recovered from a shipwreck of circa 1400 to 1375 BC weigh around 60 pounds, about the same as the ancient light talent of the Mediterranean; those from a later wreck around 1250 to 1150 BC weigh about 10 percent less.[28] Ingots found on Crete and elsewhere are of variable weight, both heavier and lighter.

Bronze, in the form of rough lumps called *aes rude* (and later as both unmarked and marked bars), was the earliest money of ancient Rome, from the eighth century BC or before to the third century. It passed by weight, with one *as* weighing one Roman *libra*, 11-1/2 ounces.[29]

From 449 BC or earlier, Roman law prescribed that the sale of slaves, beasts, land, and rural easements was to take place in the presence of at least five witnesses and a *libripens*, the

Aes rude (actual size)

man who held the scales to weigh the bronze lumps.[30] When army pay was introduced between circa 400 and 340 BC, it was called *stipendium*, "an amount weighed out."[31]

Swedish Plate Money

Swedish 10-daler plate
(actual size: 70 cm x 30 cm)

Like ancient Cyprus, Sweden was blessed with huge supplies of copper. In 1644 it was decided to "mint" some of it into enormous 10 *daler* "coins" weighing about 48 pounds each. These cumbersome rectangles resemble Cypriot ox-hide ingots without the legs and are not much lighter. This monstrosity was dropped in 1645, but 8-daler pieces were made from 1652 to 1682, 3 and 5 dalers in 1674, 4 dalers from 1649 to 1768, 1 and 2 dalers from 1649 to 1776, and 1/2 dalers (weighing close to 2 pounds themselves) from 1681 to 1776. Dates later than 1768 are unknown, as the last pieces were made from old dies.[32] Copper plate money was unsuccessfully copied by Russia between 1725 and 1727.[33]

Gold

Gold was adopted for monetary use after silver and copper. By the 15th century BC it was used in Egypt and had largely replaced silver as a medium of exchange in

Mesopotamia and Elam.[34] Gold rings are mentioned in the Bible in the bride-price of Rebekah: "the man took a gold nose ring of half a shekel weight, and two bracelets for her hands of ten shekels weight of gold" (Gen. 24:22), and in the restoration of the fortunes of Job, "every man also gave him a piece of money *[qesitah]*, and every one [a] ring of gold" (Job 42:11). Pre-coinage gold, however, has been excavated at only a single site in Israel (Gezer), in the form of a small, elongated ingot with the ends cut off and a smaller oval lump.[35]

Gold nuggets

The ancient Greeks held gold to be precious also; Homer ranked it highly for prizes and the presentation of esteemed gifts.[36] A late-eighth-century hoard of *hackgold*, similar to Middle Eastern hacksilver hoards, was found below the floor of a house in Eretria, Greece.[37] The legend of the Golden Fleece is thought to be based on an expedition of circa 1200 to circa 1000 BC to seize gold dust washed out of river sands with the aid of sheepskins, in the region of Armenia.[38]

Other rich deposits were in the lands of the Aegean, Persia, and Lydia in western Anatolia. The stream Pactolus, which flowed into the river Hermus, carried large amounts of gold dust down from the north side of Mt. Tmolus. The Lydians are said to have collected some of this gold in sheepskins spread in the shallows.[39] The rest was obtained by washing the gold-bearing sand and mud. A Lydian would partly fill a wooden bowl and, standing knee-deep in the Pactolus, add some water and swirl the contents around, allowing the water and lighter particles to escape over the rim. The heavier gold dust was then picked out by hand.[40] This source gave Lydian king Kroisos (Croesus) his wealth and led to the proverbial "as rich as Croesus."[41]

Africa has always been rich in gold too. The West African kingdom of Ghana was already known as "the land of gold" by about AD 734, though the gold actually came from a district to the south. The supply there was so great that gold was traded weight for weight for salt. Later, Ghana was absorbed into the empire of Mali, whose ruler Mansa Musa was famous for his pilgrimage to Mecca in 1324. Surrounded

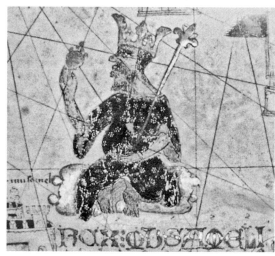

Mansa Musa

by an entourage and caravans of camels bearing gifts, he was mounted on a horse and preceded by 500 slaves, each bearing a staff of gold. Mansa Musa made presents of so much gold that in Egypt its value had not recovered even 12 years later.[42]

Gold dust–seeking traders from Mali settled among the Akan peoples in Ashanti in the 13th or 14th century.[43] From the beginning of the 18th century to about 1914, gold dust was the only money in use there, weighed with every transaction.[44]

Raw gold became currency in 19th-century America as well. During the Georgia gold rush of 1829 and later, the going price for a drink was roughly the amount of gold dust that would lie on the point of a knife.[45] Soon after gold was discovered in California on January 24, 1848, gold dust passed at $16 an ounce.[46] In 1849, "if a man entered a store to make a purchase," said the *San Francisco Alta California*, "he drew from his pocket a long leathern purse and in payment for the slightest thing, out from the long, wrinkled, twisted neck poured the rich fine gold in flakes."[47] The smallest denomination in use was the "pinch"—the amount of gold dust the seller could raise between his thumb and forefinger.[48]

Prospecting for gold

Gold dust circulated in the gold regions of the American West, including Alaska, as late as the early 1900s. It was also the sole currency in gold-producing regions of Asia until early in the 20th century.[49] As recently as 1988, gold dust was the only money used in Porto Velho, Brazil, located in the gold region of the Amazon rain forest; prices were calculated in grams.[50]

Iron

By about 1200 BC, weapons and tools of bronze in the Near East and southeast Europe had been largely replaced by those of iron. Over the next few centuries, the so-called Iron Age spread west throughout the balance of Europe. In the British Isles, the Iron Age extended from the fifth century BC until the Roman conquest, and still later in non-Romanized parts.[51]

British iron currency bars
(20% actual size)

According to Plutarch, Lycurgus introduced iron bars weighing one Eubœan *mina* (almost 1 pound) each as the sole currency of Sparta, circa 825 BC;[52] however, Lycurgus' dates and deeds are very doubtful. Elsewhere in ancient Greece, iron oxen-roasting spits *(obelos)* up to about 5 feet long, originally given as offerings to temples, were current; they remained so even after the introduction of silver coins; six spits made a *drachme* (a "graspful"), later a silver *drachma* coin.[53]

When Julius Caesar invaded Britain in 54 BC, he reported that the Britons had iron money: "They use as money either bronze or gold coins or iron bars of fixed weight."[54] Iron currency bars of this era have been found throughout southwest Britain and along nearby trading routes. They are about 2 feet long and resemble unfinished swords; their weights are apparently on a scale of 1/4, 1/2, 1, 2, and 4 units.[55]

In modern times, iron currencies of fixed size or weight were also used in Assam, Brunei, and Laos.[56]

Ancient Briton
with currency bar

USEFUL ARTICLES

As civilization progressed, barter developed in other useful articles besides raw materials. Soon these too became measures of value as well as media of exchange, in some cases becoming actual legal tender.

AGRICULTURAL ITEMS

Ankole cattle

Livestock

Domestic animals were an indicator of wealth and a medium of exchange in ancient Israel: "And Abram was very rich in livestock, in silver, and in gold." (Gen. 13:2); Abraham paid Abimelech seven ewe lambs to be a witness that he dug the well at Beersheba (Gen. 21:30); and Judah agreed to pay one kid to a harlot as the price of her services (Gen. 38:15–17).

Among the ancient Greeks, the standard was oxen. Homer sang that the armor of Diomedês cost only nine oxen, while that of Glaucos cost a hundred oxen.[1] A large tripod was valued by the Achaeans at 12 oxen, and a skilled slave woman at four.[2] Cattle were also the earliest currency in ancient Rome; the Latin word for money, *pecunia*, was derived from *pecus*, cattle. One head of cattle was equal to 10 sheep.[3]

Cattle currency survived in Caucasia even after the introduction of Russian money, among the Chefsurs and Ossetes; the Ossetes even reckoned in fractions of a cow, one cow being worth 10 sheep or five rubles.[4]

Camels, sheep, and goats—but chiefly cows—were the standard of value in north, east, and southern Africa for millennia. They were spent only for bride-price or fines; in 19th-century Bechuanaland, 10 head of cattle would usually purchase a wife. Until well into the 20th century, cattle were the principal currency among the Masai of Kenya, and old and diseased cows had the same value as young, healthy ones.[5]

Geography influenced the choice of animal. In pre-Islamic Arabia, the standard "blood money" *(diya)* required for murder was the payment of a hundred camels to the victim's tribe,[6] while in frigid northern Siberia, it was the domesticated reindeer that was the medium of exchange. As late as the 19th century, buffalo were the monetary unit among the tribes of Annam. Pigs were widely used as money throughout Oceania, and are still part of the bride-price in Papua New Guinea.[7] In rural Cambodia, bundles of live chickens tied at the feet were used for major purchases as recently as 2005.[8]

Trobriand Island boar

Eggs and Grain

Durable foodstuffs served as money in pastoral states over the centuries. Eggs were used as small change in many places; they were accepted by the Nauru Island post office for stamps in the early 1900s, and still circulate in rural Guatemala.[9]

In Babylonia, barley began to be used as money prior to 1926 BC, and the Code of Hammurabi monetized it and fixed its value to silver; however, the barley/silver ratio had to be adjusted frequently, and barley was so unpopular with merchants that the death penalty was decreed for those who refused to accept it.[10]

In the Hittite Empire, a 14th-century BC law code prescribed payments in measures of barley, in addition to weighed silver.[11] Grain was a currency in ancient China and was actually made legal tender in AD 24.[12] Bags of oats or barley circulated in ancient Ireland.[13]

Rice was used for small payments in 13th-century Cambodia and in Japan until the 18th century; in French Indochina, the principal tax was payable in rice. In Burma in the 20th century, only inferior rice remained in circulation, as the better quality was eaten.[14] Bitter almonds were small change in Sudan and India from the Middle Ages until the past century, though in India only those unfit for human consumption were spent.[15]

Maize (Indian corn) was used as money in Guatemala, Mexico, and colonial New England. In Guatemala, the unit was a gourdful weighing about a pound, which was worth one peso as recently as the mid-20th century. In 1640 Indian corn was made legal tender in Massachusetts at the rate of 4 shillings a bushel and continued to circulate at various rates into the 18th century.[16]

Maize

SLAVES

Slavery was well established by the third millennium BC, and by the late second millennium slaves had acquired quasi-monetary status in Greece; Homer wrote that Agamemnon offered seven slave women, among other valuables, in an effort to appease Achilles (late 13th century BC).[17]

Irish Slave Girls

In ancient Ireland, the slave girl or bondsmaid (*kumal*) became a monetary unit, though the *kumal* perhaps morphed into an abstract unit of account as early as the second century AD. In the pre-Christian epic *Táin Bó Cúailnge*, Queen Medb's chariot is said to be worth 21 kumals. Each kumal equaled three cows.[18]

Irish slave girl

Ba-na "Heads"

In the late 19th century, the *Ba-na* (Bahnar) of Annam, who lived in what is now the Central Highlands provinces of Vietnam, had as their highest unit the "head," i.e., a male slave. However, it had a variable value, depending on the slave's age, strength, and skill; one head was worth either five, six, or seven buffaloes.[19]

African Slaves

Slaves were money throughout much of Africa. V.L. Cameron, who was sent by the Royal Geographical Society to assist Dr. Livingstone, wrote of his efforts to buy canoes at Nyangwe on the Lualaba River in August 1874:

African slaves

At the first [market] that occurred after my arrival, I found cowries, goats, and slaves were the only currency available in large purchases; and being without these, I could do no *trade* . . . I tried every means to persuade the people to sell me canoes, but without avail. [Some] said they would bring canoes if I paid for them in slaves; but I replied that, as an Englishman, I could not deal in slaves . . . [One chief agreed to accept cowries in lieu of slaves at the current price, but reneged], remarking that if he took home such a quantity of cowries they would only be appropriated by his wives as ornaments, and he would be poorer by a canoe; and his wives wearing numbers of cowries would not provide him with better food or clothing.

So anxious was I to close this bargain, that I offered double the value of his canoe in cowries, saying that surely his wives could not possibly wear such an amount.

But he had a wonderfully keen idea of trading, and replied that the cowries would be lying idle and bringing him in nothing till he managed to buy slaves with them, whereas if he received slaves in payment he could set them at work at once to paddle canoes between the markets, to catch fish, to make pottery, or to cultivate his fields; in fact, he did not want his capital to lie idle.[20]

TOOLS AND WEAPONS

Essential tools and weapons for hunting, fishing, agriculture, and food preparation were desirable barter items from early times. In some cases, standard patterns—sometimes in token form—became money.

Stone Axes and Blades

In pre-colonial New Zealand, the Maori used nephrite adzes to buy ritual performances and funerals and compensate for crimes.[21] Ceremonial axe blades could purchase pigs, canoes, land, even sorcery in the Trobriand Islands into the 20th century.[22] Tribes in Irian Jaya (West Papua) used stone axes for bride-price as late as the 1980s.[23]

Stone axe head (40% actual size)

Bronze and Iron Axes

Bronze double axes, which had religious significance in the Minoan culture during the second millennium BC, occur in hoards throughout Central Europe. These, and similarly-shaped ingots, were certainly valuable religious offerings and probably currency also.[24]

More convincing as currency are the looped, socketed axe heads found from the Balkans to Ireland, dating to circa 1200 to circa 700 BC and later. Some pieces are too small for actual use; a single deposit at Maure-de-Bretagne, Dép. Ille-et-Vilaine, Normandy, contained 4,000 pieces that were only about 2 inches

Bronze socketed axe head (actual size)

long. More than 100 hoards of these miniature axe heads have been recovered in Albania alone: 124 of these and similar types dating to the 10th century BC were found at Torovica.[25]

Iron axes and blades, including nonfunctional types, were used as money by many African tribes. Axes were also used as money in Middle Tennessee in pioneer days, around 1789 to 1810; a 640 acre tract of land near Nashville was once sold for "three axes and two cow-bells."[26]

Native American Copper Currency Axes

About AD 800 to 900, the Indians of coastal Ecuador began hammering out small copper-alloy axe heads—stackable, but too thin for actual use—for use as money. These *hachas monedas* (currency axes) were usually bundled in groups of five, 10, and 20; in addition to the main denomination, 3 inches long, two smaller sizes, including a miniature only about 1 inch long, were made later. By circa 1400 they were obsolete.[27]

Trade from Ecuador north along the Pacific Coast introduced hachas monedas to the natives of Mesoamerica, and they were imitated in western Mexico beginning about 1200 to 1300 in the form of chisel-shaped pieces with just a slight fanning at the end, beaten almost paper thin.[28]

North Andean currency axes (actual sizes)

Aztec god depicted on Codex Laud (actual size)

Mexican axe (65% actual size)

Similar copper axes are illustrated in a number of 16th- or 17th-century native codices. The 16th-century Aztec Codex Laud shows an axe-wielding figure while the Codex Mendoza shows fan-shaped axes, both affixed to a club-like handle and as an isolated blade, associated with tribute and merchants. The Madrid Codex (Mayan) shows the merchant god Ek-Chuah holding a wedge-shaped copper axe hafted near the end of a simple club-shaped handle.[29]

As the use of currency axes in Mexico spread east and south, other forms were adopted, all somewhat thicker and with raised ridges along the sides of the shank. In Oaxaca, they were primarily shaped like a *tau* or mushroom cross section, but three other types were made also. Sizes vary from miniatures of 1 inch to huge pieces up to 14 inches long. In 1528, 113 cases of such axes were among the tribute stored in the arsenal in Mexico City.[30]

Mexican axes (65% actual size)

Copper currency axes became an accepted form of money in Mexico among both natives and Spanish. They acquired an exchange rate in coins: by 1548, according to a letter written from Oaxaca, "these were commonly accepted [at] four such pieces, if new, for five Spanish *reales*. When slightly worn, they were rejected, and then they were sold to be melted at 10 pieces for one Spanish *real*."[31] Perhaps the 92 percent devaluation when worn was due to the axes losing a high polish that made them appear to be gold. They passed out of circulation about 1600.

Anchor-shaped Mexican axe (65% actual size)

Most axes have been found in the western coastal states of Mexico, chiefly the state of Oaxaca, though they were also used in Colima, Michoacán, and Guerrero to the north, and as far east as Honduras. They have sometimes been found in large hoards. About 1833, an Indian plowed up an earthen pot containing 276 "anchor"-shaped pieces half a mile from the city of Oaxaca near Monte Alban, evidently buried centuries before. During the empire of Maximilian, several wagonloads of axe money were brought into Oaxaca and melted for bullets to use against the French. In 1910, an American discovered 327 pieces in a tomb on Monte Alban in layers of four, with the cutting edges facing outward to form a cross.[32]

Chinese Spade Money

Bronze was much admired in ancient China, used for vessels, implements, and weapons. Whether bronze spades themselves became barter items in early times is disputed, though it seems likely.[33] In any case, cast miniature spades (*bù*) with pointed corners were made for currency use in north-central China circa 770 to 221 BC. (Note: very early dates for their introduction are given in older works, but modern Chinese numismatists accept a date in the Spring and Autumn

Chinese spade money
(above and right: actual size)

Wang Mang spade
money (actual size)

period, between 770 and 476 BC, since the first regulations for the weight of spade and knife money occur about 670 to 665 BC.) The earliest pieces have hollow handles with reinforcing ribs like real spades and lack inscriptions; they are nearly 6 inches long and probably suitable for agriculture.[34]

Most later examples, cast to a reduced weight standard of about 30 grams, omitted the unnecessary hollow handle and added brief inscriptions. In the final stages, sizes and weights were greatly reduced, holes for stringing were added, and they became so stylized that someone not seeing the prior forms would wonder why they were called spade money.[35]

Spade money was briefly revived by the usurper Wang Mang, circa AD 20, who cast a series of denominations from "100" to "1600."[36]

Chinese Knife Money

According to legend, on the eve of an expedition circa 679 to 675 BC, the soldiers of Duke Huan of Qi complained about having to pay fines for slight offenses with copper ring money. Their general, afraid of disloyalty and wishing to facilitate enlistment, let them use their bronze knives instead. The people were delighted with the innovation, we are told, and eagerly adopted knives as a medium of exchange.[37]

Though this story (recorded 500 years after the event) may be apocryphal, the first knife-shaped coins, probably introduced in the seventh century BC, do somewhat resemble ancient Chinese knives: a knife excavated from a pre-1122 BC site is only a little longer than early knife coins and also has a slightly curved blade with a ring on the end, though it lacks the reinforcing ribs.

The earliest issues have long inscriptions stating their origin; later pieces are smaller and simpler. All are cast in bronze. The last major series, Ming (the legend seems to read *ming* knife, though the meaning of ming is uncertain), made between circa 390 and

Chinese knife money (actual size)

280 BC, adds inscriptions indicating the location of the mold in the furnace. The final knife coins were diminutive, key-like pieces issued by Wang Mang.

Classic knife coins mostly circulated in different areas than spade money: north and northeastern China, Korea, and even Japan.[38]

Iron Hoes

Various kinds of iron hoes were a form of money in many parts of sub-Saharan Africa. In Nigeria in the 1850s, 40 hoes would buy a slave. Around 1921, the Madi tribe of northern Uganda even made special anchor-shaped "marriage hoes"—too large for practical use—solely for bride-price payments.[39]

Iron "marriage hoe" (30% actual size)

Arrowheads

Scythian arrowheads were apparently used as money in the western Black Sea area during the seventh to the fifth century BC. Greek colonists in Borysthenes, Olbia, and Thrace cast huge numbers of stylized copies of them between circa 525 and 350 BC for monetary purposes, though leaving off the sharp point for easier handling.[40]

Thrace arrowhead money
(actual size)

Fishhooks

Pearl shell fishhooks were used as currency, gifts to chiefs, and offerings to gods in the Gilbert and Ellis Islands in the 1890s. Fishhook money also circulated in the Marshall and Solomon Islands in the early 20th century; there it consisted of

Fishhook money (actual size)

serviceable-looking hooks, but nearby in the eastern Caroline Islands, the series passed from the backs of fishhooks (without hooks, though called *ka muäk*, "fishhook money") to breast ornaments (called *fae metmet*) with no obvious break.[41]

Guns and Ammunition

Guns, more specifically muskets or rifles, were a necessity on the frontier. From the late 17th through the 19th century, traders bought furs from Tlingit and Haida natives on the northwest coast of North America with flintlock trade guns, marked in later years by a trademark of a sea-serpent or dragon on the side-screw plate. At one time the Hudson's Bay Company exchanged one gun for 20 "made

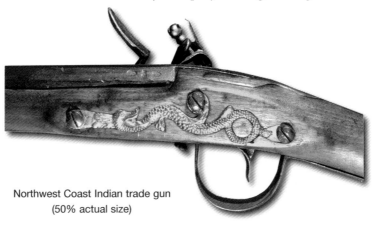

Northwest Coast Indian trade gun
(50% actual size)

beaver" (a pelt worn for at least one season, from which most of the long outer hair not used for hat-making had worn off). Trade guns were readily accepted by Indians inland from the coast.[42]

Goods in the region of the lower Congo were priced in guns by 1879. Though actual guns were a medium of exchange, the "gun" was primarily a standard of value to facilitate barter; each "gun" represented a certain assortment of trade goods.[43]

In 1635, Massachusetts decreed that "muskett bulletts of a full boare shall pass currently for a farthing apieece," up to one shilling. In the 17th century, a standard English musket fired a huge ball weighing 1-1/3 ounces, so a shilling's worth of them equaled 4 pounds of lead.[44] The Hudson's Bay Company also traded powder and shot.[45]

Musket ball (actual size)

VESSELS

Wooden Bowls

Wooden bowls turned by pioneer settler Judge Alexander L. Ely at the sawmill in money-starved Allegan, Michigan, then a small village, served as small change in 1840.[46]

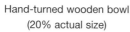
Hand-turned wooden bowl
(20% actual size)

Pots

Pots were made in Papua New Guinea for currency use as well as cooking and storage. Many villages specialized in pottery for trade and bride-price payments.[47] Among some Negrito tribes of New Guinea, pots were a standard of value early in the 20th century. The price of a wife was 10 pots—the value of the girl's labor for three years.[48] But the Sio people would sell a dog or a pig for the same 10 pots; a single pot was worth two to four coconuts. The Jitibu people formerly sold their canoes for 20 pots, and a large fish for four pots. In the Murik Lakes area, a single pot would purchase 50 to 150 pounds of taro, depending on its size.

In New Britain, most pots made in former times were wealth and trade items, though some were actually used for cooking. In the 1960s, the price of a dog or pig was 10 pots; more recently, a piglet can be purchased for two pots.[49] Pots are still used as bride-price payments in western New Britain and on Umboi Island.[50]

Pot from Papua New Guinea
(25% actual size)

On Tubetube Island, a single pot would buy six yams, a bunch of bananas, or a bunch of areca nuts. Commerce using pots was conducted on a large scale across the Vitiaz Strait, with huge canoes carrying a cargo of 200 to 300 clay pots to the Sio and other peoples.[51]

GARMENT NEEDS

Furs

Among societies dependent upon hunting wild animals, furs and skins became currency. In 1876, economist William Stanley Jevons wrote,

> Perhaps the most rudimentary state of industry is that in which subsistence is gained by hunting wild animals. The proceeds of the chase would, in such a state, be the property of most generally recognized value. The meat of the animals captured would,

Marten pelt

indeed, be too perishable in nature to be hoarded or often exchanged; but it is otherwise with the skins, which, being preserved and valued for clothing, became one of the earliest materials of currency. Accordingly, there is abundant evidence that furs or skins were employed as money in many ancient nations. They serve this purpose to the present day in some parts of the world.[52]

In Siberia, some tribes used furs for tax payments and bride-price a late as World War I.[53] Members of the weasel family were often desired: the Volga Bulgars used marten skins for small change,[54] and in 1313 Venice imposed an annual tax of 3,000 marten skins on Zadar, in modern-day Croatia;[55] the marten *(kuna)* also gave its name to the monetary unit of Croatia. Sable pelts were a legal pledge in 15th century Poland. In Siberia, Tungus tribe prostitutes were paid in ermine skins.[56] And the "lost" State of Franklin (eastern Tennessee) passed a law in 1788 making one mink skin the fee of a constable for serving a warrant.[57]

Squirrel pelts could be spent in northern Eurasia from the Baltic coast to Siberia until the 13th century, and even later in Asia. Bear skins were made legal tender in French Canada in 1673, while otter skins circulated in Alaska and British Columbia in early days. Raccoon pelts were used as money in Kentucky and Tennessee in the 18th century. Even fur scraps such as ears and claws were used as money in medieval Russia, replacing scarcer whole skins, until Mongol invaders rejected them as worthless in the 13th century.[58]

In North America, beaver skins were the most generally accepted: some Indians believed beaver to be sacred,[59] and there was strong demand for beaver pelts in Europe to make hats.[60] They became the standard against which the values of other pelts were measured.[61] In a 1703 price list, all Indian goods were priced in beavers, even if other skins were tendered.[62] In Canada, the Hudson's Bay Company established the "made beaver" as the standard of value soon after 1670, and it remained in use until the 1850s.[63] In Massachusetts, Native American Chickataubott was "fyned a skyn of beauer for shooteinge a swine" in 1631, and Dutch bricks were sold in New Amsterdam in 1661 for $4.16 per thousand, payable in beaver skins.[64] As late as 1788, each county clerk in the State of Franklin was to be paid 300 beaver skins as an annual salary.[65]

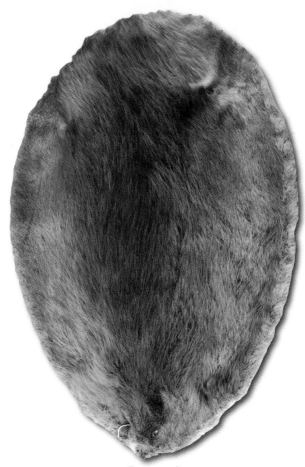

Beaver pelt

Skins

While moose hides were made legal tender in French Canada in 1674,[66] buck-skins were a virtually universal currency in North America in the 18th and 19th centuries. They were familiarly called "bucks": Indian negotiator Conrad Weiser informed a council in Ohio on September 17, 1748, "Every [cask] of Whiskey shall be sold to you for 5 Bucks in your town."[67]

As a buckskin was generally worth a dollar then, the slang term "buck" for dollar apparently originated on the American frontier some time in the 18th century. When Illinois frontiersman William Biggs was captured by Kickapoo Indians on March 27, 1788, and held for ransom, he wrote later in a letter to his brother: "My price was 107 bucks or dollars."[68] Buckskins were actually made a legal tender by the State of Franklin in 1785 at the equivalent of one dollar apiece.[69] Farther north, in Highland County, Ohio, around 1800 to 1803, bucks

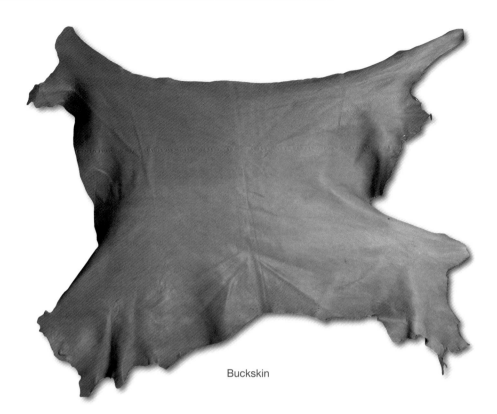

Buckskin

could be used to buy salt, at the rate of $4 or four buckskins for 50 pounds.[70] Buckskins circulated on the frontier until circa 1840.

Woven Cloth

Because of its utility for garments, woven cloth was used in payment in Egypt (linen)[71] and China (silk and hemp) as early as the second millennium BC. In fact, the Chinese word *bù*, originally "cloth," subsequently also meant "money." During the sixth century BC, a Chinese prince actually refused payment in coins on one occasion in favor of silk.[72] Cloth money was used sporadically in China until the 17th century.[73]

In the Middle Ages, woven cloth circulated in Northern and Eastern Europe. Traveler Ibrahim ben Ya'qub observed net-like cloths of half-moon shapes during his visit to Bohemia in 965: "They . . . possess entire jars of them," he wrote. "For them, they are money and the most precious thing with which one can buy wheat, flour, horses, gold, silver, and all the rest." Worth 1/10 of a silver denar, they permitted it to be changed.[74] In some districts of Sweden as late as the 14th century, home-woven woolen cloth was actually legal tender and had an exchange rate with coins similar to that in Bohemia.[75] Cloth money, as a measure of value at least, survived in parts of Iceland until the 19th century.[76]

Aztec cotton mantles

In the Western Hemisphere, cotton textiles were a form of money for trade and tax payments among the Incas, Aztecs, and Mayas as late as 1549.[77] The Aztecs used *patolquechtli*, small squares of cotton fabric, as money in some areas. Large mantles, called *quachtli*, were valuable as well. A single quachtli could purchase a canoe, while 30 would buy a slave.[78] Emperor Motecuhzoma Xocoyotzin (1502–1520) received an incredible 2,000,000 cotton mantles in tax payments each year.[79]

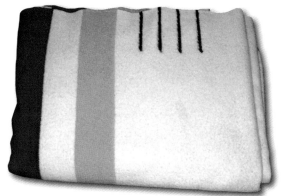

Hudson's Bay blanket

Woolen blankets of the Hudson's Bay Company became the principal currency in their area by the middle of the 19th century: in 1859, two blankets would buy a gun. Besides commerce, these blankets circulated in two irregular ways, a gambling game played with sticks and through the potlatch. This unique custom, ostensibly an act of magnanimity, was in reality often a challenge hurled through the medium of gifts. On the principle of reciprocal giving, one showered one's rival with costly gifts; if he accepted them, he must give a better potlatch in return. And if he could not afford to accept them, he was disgraced and the potlatch-giver won.

Tribesmen of the Northwest Coast spent their whole lives preparing for their potlatch, and woolen blankets were the chief currency. At the age of 10, each boy began his adult life with a credit of 100 blankets. He then devoted the rest of his life to amassing blankets, by lending at 100 percent interest, earning Canadian money through commercial salmon fishing, etc., so that he could become wealthy enough to challenge a rival from a different tribe selected for him.[80] When the time came, thousands of blankets—in low piles so that they covered a considerable amount of ground[81]—and other European goods including motorboats and sewing machines, were distributed over a period of several days, accompanied by great feasting. The potlatch reached the height of its development under the Southern Kwakiutl from 1849 to 1925, but had virtually ceased by the 1960s.[82]

In Africa, native cloth money was used by tribes from Angola to Ethiopia, woven from local fibrous plants.[83] Lele tribesmen in the Congo (Kuba kingdom) used leaves of the raffia palm to weave *madiba*, which was used as money before the arrival of white traders. The need for madiba

Madiba cloth

was constant, as a skirt made from it wore out in about four months. Ten lengths would buy an axe or—as late as the 1930s—90 to 100 lengths, a slave.[84]

Imported cotton cloth was widely used as money all over sub-Saharan Africa, reckoned by the "piece," a unit of variable size. Generally, only rolls or bolts of imported cloth were money; cuttings of the same cloth were not, but in the 1880s and 1890s, Congo pygmies accepted red cotton handkerchiefs in payment, and the Bigirmi of Nigeria used whole shirts in the 1850s, including little shirts too small to wear, made for monetary use only.[85]

Small pieces of cotton cloth circulated in parts of Indonesia from the 15th century to about 1900. The farther islands, including Sumba, Flores, Timor, Bali, and Sulawesi used *ikat*, a native woven cloth, for bride-price and other payments and as a store of value. In central Sulawesi, large pieces were used to pay fines and make peace, though

Ikat cloth

they were seldom worn as clothing. On Sumba, payment of *ikat* was essential in order to incorporate a wife and her offspring into her husband's clan. Each area had its own design.[86]

Pacific Island Bark Cloth

Bark cloth, a paperlike fabric, was the chief material for clothing of both sexes throughout Oceania. It originated in China as early as 5000 BC, and the ancient Chinese names, *tha-pu (tapu, tafu)* and *ka-pu*, have survived today as *tapa* and *kapa*.[87] Over time, it became a medium of exchange in some islands and, to a lesser extent, a store of value.[88]

By 1925, when Margaret Mead did her famous field work on Samoa, production was declining: "The use of some money and of cloth, purchased from traders, has freed women from part of the immense labor of manufacturing mats and tapa as units of exchange and for clothing."[89] Small bits of Samoan tapa were worth only a shilling or two, while those of mosquito screen size were valued at four or five dollars.[90]

Tongan canoes brought large sheets of bark cloth to Fiji hundreds of years ago to purchase sandalwood; a Fijian rated his wealth by the amount of bark cloth he possessed, whether piled up in his hut or wound around and around his body.[91] As late as 1959, bark cloth figured in an exchange ritual to purchase mats in Tonga at a rate of about 20 sheets of cloth per mat.[92] In the Marquesas prior to 1920, it was part of the payment required for tattooing the first-born son.[93]

Tapa cloth

OTHER EDIBLES

Bread

In the markets of 11th-century Baghdad, loaves of bread were spent as if they were silver coins, though those that were moldy or had broken edges were rejected. Quoted al-Maqrīzī, "As for bread, its dough is left exposed at the front of the store and swarms of flies flock to it. It is then baked in ovens filled with smoke. These [flat] loaves are then [taken out] extremely dry [and crisp]. People use them as a medium of exchange

Iraq bread market

in the markets. . . . They use the loaves in purchasing most of their food and per-
fume, and in paying the [fee for the] public bath. This same [bread] is accepted by
wine merchants, tavern owners, cloth merchants, and perfumers."[94]

Loaves and grain also served as a means of payment in Denmark at about the
same time, and the prices of all commodities were fixed in terms of barley or rye
as late as the 14th century.[95]

Olive Oil

Olive oil is fairly uniform in quality (by grade), durable, and easily
divisible. From circa 1400 into the
20th century, extra virgin olive oil
was money in the little hilltop village of Mošćenice, Croatia; work-
ers at the olive press were paid in
olive oil. The mayor was also paid
in olive oil, and 10 percent was
given to the church. Local production was discontinued in 1979.[96]

Olive oil was used as currency
for centuries in the Greek Islands
as well. During the huge inflation
at the end of World War II, it was
adopted (with wheat) as a standard
of value to facilitate barter
throughout all Greece.[97]

Olive oil press, Mošćenice

Salt

Salt was used as money in Asia, Africa, America, and Oceania. Marco Polo discovered it being used for small change in the province of Kain-Du in Mongol China
circa 1275 to 1292: "In this country there are salt-springs, from which they manufacture salt by boiling it in small pans. When the water has boiled for an hour, it
becomes a kind of paste, which is formed into cakes . . . flat on the lower side and
convex on the upper." The stamp of the Grand Khan was then impressed. Each salt
cake was worth 1/480 ounce of gold at the springs, but much more at a distance.[98]
As late as 1921, salt was used as currency by tribes in Viet Nam, Siam, and Burma.[99]

By 1526, salt circulated in Ethiopia in the form of thick rock-salt blocks
6 inches long. At the source, each block had little value, but as it traveled farther,
it became worth nearly its weight in gold and would purchase a slave. In the
1930s four sizes were made, and to make change they were divided into halves
and quarters.[100] Salt blocks were the only currency in particularly undeveloped

Ethiopian salt bar (60% actual size)

regions of Ethiopia as of 1948, and they still circulate now.[101] It was a courtesy there, when meeting a friend, to proffer a salt bar to be licked. Thus one's money was diminished through hospitality![102]

Salt is still quarried from rock-salt deposits at Taoudenni in the Sahara Desert, as it has been since prehistoric times. Even now, the salt caravans continue; an Associated Press story dated January 7, 2001, reported that—though partially superseded by trucks—camels loaded with four 80-pound blocks each still made the trek from Taoudenni to Timbuktu monthly, and the salt miners were paid in salt.[103] Rock salt wrapped in tree leaves was also used as money in

Salt caravan

Angola, another source, from the 16th through the 19th century.[104]

Katanga salt bar (15% actual size)

Salt bars called *dibanda*, weighing 6-1/2 pounds, were used in the Katanga region of the Congo. In Nigeria, local brines were boiled in pots to make salt cones, which passed for currency there and in Cameroon.[105] The Limba tribe of Sierra Leone used salt packed solidly in narrow baskets more than 2 feet long, sealed with mud, into the 1950s or 1960s; most recently, the usual bride-price was 10 baskets of salt.[106]

In Chiapas, Mexico, from pre-Columbian times until the 20th century, the Lacandon Mayas used salt money made by burning palm trees.[107] Pre-Inca and Inca groups traded salt too, and as late as 1949 the Indians of Otavalo Valley, Ecuador, used salt as a medium of exchange.[108] Salt also circulated in Borneo and Oceania, and some tribes in Papua New Guinea were still using salt money in the mid-1960s.[109]

Sierra Leone salt basket
(15% actual size)

Pepper

Pepper was an important article of trade between India and Europe in antiquity, so much so that it became a medium of exchange. Tributes were levied in pepper in ancient Greece and Rome.[110] Alaric the Visigoth was persuaded to raise his siege of Rome in AD 408 for 5,000 pounds of gold, 30,000 pounds of silver, 4,000 silk robes, 3,000 pieces of fine scarlet cloth—and 3,000 pounds of pepper.[111]

Peppercorns (actual size)

Customs duties in medieval Germany were often payable in wine, cheese, herring, or pepper.[112] In Poland, Boleslaus the Pious (1239–1279), duke of Greater Poland, encouraged Jews to settle in Poland in large numbers, granting special rights to them in 1264 by the Statutes of Kalisz. Statute 16 states: "If a Jew has been condemned by his judge to pay the fine known as *Wandel*, he shall pay his judge a talent of pepper which is the anciently established fine."[113] Pepper continued to be legal tender for taxes on the Baltic Sea coast as late as the 15th and 16th centuries, at the rate of 10 peppercorns to the Baltic silver schilling.[114]

Pepper was a standard of value in Italy too during the Middle Ages. Between 1075 and 1140, an equivalent for a sum of money to be paid in Lombardy was stipulated in pepper. In 1378, Genoa issued a pepper loan, repayable either in pepper or in gold at the holder's option.[115]

Pepper was a means of payment at the source as well. In the early 17th century, pepper money was used in a district of Sumatra, according to Chinese author Tung Hli Yung K'An: "When the men of Jambi bargain for goods, the price is agreed upon in gold, but they pay only in pepper, e.g., if something costs two taels of gold, they pay a hundred *piculs* of pepper or thereabouts. They like to buy foreign women, and girls from other countries are often brought here and sold for pepper."[116]

Jambi was merely the port of shipment; traders from there traveled to the interior by boat to buy the pepper. The trade was dominated by women, and elite women of the court were the only ones with connections to the pepper-growing districts. Consequently, good relations between the upstream and downstream communities were essential for pepper exports, and the Southeast Asians only trusted people who were kin to them. As a result, 17th-century Chinese pepper buyers usually married local women, which ritually transformed them into kin of the Sumatrans.

All this began to change in 1619 with the arrival of the Dutch East India Company. Misunderstanding the kinship-trade system, the Dutch treated women offered to them as wives like prostitutes. Thus they had to hire Chinese middlemen to buy the pepper, and the Dutch pepper monopoly slipped away. By 1768 the Dutch post at Jambi was closed.[117]

Cacao Beans

Seeds of the cacao tree (pronounced ka-ków), commonly referred to as "beans," were in general use as money in Central America for centuries. Originally, cacao beans were used to make a foamed cocoa drink. But unlike today, the drinking of cocoa was restricted to the royal family, favored elites, and soldiers—because for common people to drink cocoa would be to "urinate their money away."[118]

Cultivation of cacao may have begun as early as 1000 BC, and it became an extremely important commodity after about AD 250. By AD 900 at the latest, the Mayas were using cacao beans as money.[119]

Cacao beans (actual size)

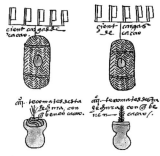

Carga of cacao beans,
Mendoza Codex

At the beginning of the 14th century, the war-like Aztecs arrived in the Valley of Mexico. Over the next century they built a great empire, claiming tribute in the form of cacao beans from neighboring tribes. The treasury / cacao warehouse of the Aztec emperor Motecuhzoma Xocoyotzin (1502–1520) held more than 40,000 *cargas*, or almost one billion beans![120] The cacao was stored in huge cubical wicker bins, coated in clay to seal the interstices between the fibers, each of which contained 600 loads—or 14,400,000 beans.[121] (The Aztecs used a vigesimal [base 20] numbering system, with *xiquipilli* [8,000, or 20 x 400 beans] equal to a "bag of cacao beans." However, 8,000 x 3 = 24,000 = 1 carga, or load for a porter.) [122]

In Nicaragua in 1535, 10 beans would buy a rabbit, 100 beans (more or less) a slave, and 8 or 10 beans, "as they agree," the services of a prostitute.[123] Prices in Mexico, where cacao was abundant, were higher than in Nicaragua: a small rabbit, 30 beans; a hare, 100 beans; a turkey egg, 3 beans; and a large tomato or a tamale, 1 bean.[124] The Spanish conquerors of Mexico continued using cacao bean currency. On June 17, 1555, the exchange rate was set at 140 beans to 1 *real*.[125]

The value of cacao beans was high enough to encourage counterfeiting. They were imitated in varnished clay, or the heart of the bean was cleaned out through a tiny hole and the hollow shell packed with earth. To detect this, the payee was careful to handle the beans individually when counting them, pressing each one with his index finger—the shell of altered beans yielded more than the shell of solid beans.[126]

Long after coins were introduced, the Indians of Guatemala continued to prefer cacao bean money.[127] In the 1880s the smallest silver coin was equal to 40 cacao beans, and monetary usage continued as late as 1923.[128]

Chocolate (Hershey® Bar)

Cacao, in the form of chocolate, returned as money at the end of World War II. In October 1945, numismatic editor Lee F. Hewitt reported his observation that Hershey bars, together with cigarettes, were universal media of exchange throughout Europe and much of the Pacific.[129]

World War II–era Hershey bars

Candy and Gum

Candy, chewing gum, and other sundries have been pressed into service as small change during coin shortages in many places. In 1975, a bus driver in Lima, Peru, tendered a handful of caramels in change for a five-sol note. The same day, another driver refused a stick of gum and a one-sol coin in payment, only to back down when outraged passengers brandished the caramels and chewing gum *they* had received in change.[130]

A similar coin shortage in Mexico in 1958 led to supermarkets making change with sticks of Adams Yucatan–brand gum in lieu of centavo coins.[131] Italy experienced a persistent coin shortage in the mid-1970s, forcing shoppers to accept change in gumdrops, toffee candy, or mints.[132]

Adams Yucatan gum (actual size)

Kyrgyzstan candy-coated gum
(actual size)

In Kyrgyzstan in 1999, change was provided in the form of bubble gum or matches; instead of the scarce one-som note, three pieces of white, candy-coated gum or two Russian aspirin tablets were tendered on different occasions in the Bishkek market.[133] Melting of coins for their nickel and chrome content caused a coin shortage that led small traders in Jamshedpur, India, to make change in toffees in 2008.[134]

Even the United States was not immune: the U.S. Mint discontinued striking copper cents in 1942 to conserve the metal for war needs, resulting in a shortage of cents until the new steel cents were released in 1943. Many stores paid out chewing gum and other 1¢ items in change.[135] About 30 years later, record high copper prices led to hoarding of cents and another shortage. Among other attempts to cope, a "hamburger joint" in Louisville, Kentucky, offered penny suckers in change in lieu of coins in 1974.[136]

Brick Tea

Tea pressed into various sized bricks was the chief currency in eastern Tibet, Mongolia, and Siberia throughout the 19th century. On October 17, 1844, Lazarist missionary Abbé M. Huc observed that "brick tea, which the Tartars receive in exchange for the products of the desert" was an article of commerce in the Inner Mongolian Chinese trading station of "Chaborté."[137] It continued to circulate in Central Asia until at least 1935. The bricks were broken apart to make tea, but only circulated intact or in packets of four; 80 bricks might buy a horse.

Tea bricks (25% actual size)

Though inferior-quality bricks contained much wood from branches, those preferred for money used well-fermented leaves almost exclusively. Different types were produced for Tibet and for Mongolia and southern Siberia. Those intended for Mongolia (more properly called tablets) contained better quality tea and had Russian inscriptions, while those for Tibet had Chinese inscriptions.

Tea bricks were stockpiled prior to the invasion of Tibet in 1950, but brick tea ceased to function as currency after the Chinese conquest. They are still manufactured in the People's Republic of China.[138]

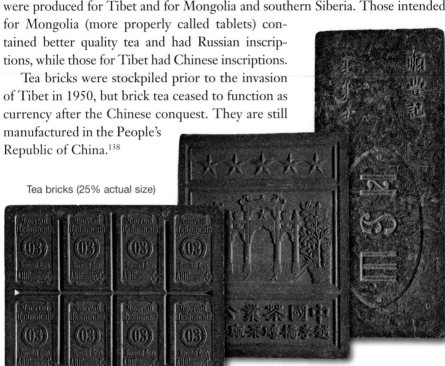

Tea bricks (25% actual size)

LIQUOR AND DRUGS
Distilled Spirits

Cheap gin, rum, and brandy were the principal media of exchange in Nigeria from the 1790s until the First World War.[139] Very frequently, bottles and even cases circulated for years without being consumed. Gin was also an excellent store of value, since it appreciated automatically with each increase in the duty on imported spirits.[140] Among the Aro people of Nigeria, marriage payments even now must include five bottles of schnapps and a bottle of whiskey.[141]

Teachers in the Altai Republic, central Russia, were paid their monthly salaries in vodka in September 1998 because of a shortage of currency. Each of the 8,000 educators received 15 bottles. (Previously they had refused payment of back wages in toilet paper.)[142] Vodka had appeared as a barter item in Russia as early as the winter of 1992, when a single bottle was then worth about as much as the weekly wages of the average worker.[143] In Poland, doctors demanded cognac in payment in 1981, though carpenters were satisfied with vodka.[144]

Gin bottles   Russian vodka   Johnny Walker Red Scotch whiskey

The cheapest variety of Antwerp gin was the standard trade currency on Tierra del Fuego during the 19th century.[145] Even in Muslim Algeria, Johnnie Walker Red Scotch whiskey was the preferred money (in place of the Algerian dinar) in 1987 for hotel rooms, gasoline, and car repairs—though it was much too valuable to actually drink.[146]

Tobacco

The English plantations in America rapidly adopted tobacco as money in the 17th century. In Bermuda, it drove the Sommer Islands Hogge Money out of circulation as soon as the first significant crop was harvested in October 1617.[147] In 1619 the General Assembly of Virginia, in its very first action, fixed the price of tobacco, already a local currency. From 1642 through 1656, tobacco was virtually the only money in Virginia, and remained important until its value collapsed in 1665 from overproduction due to the high official price.[148] Even wives could be bought with it—in 1619, "respectable girls" were sent over from England, and wife-seeking planters paid for each passage with 120 pounds of tobacco.[149] A Leeward Islands act of 1644 levied fines in terms of tobacco.[150]

While tobacco circulated in Virginia chiefly in the form of warehouse receipts, 7-inch-long twisted sticks of Virginia tobacco (sometimes flavored with licorice) were currency throughout New Guinea and much of Oceania

Tobacco sticks
(50% actual size)

from 1818 to the 1970s, though primarily used by white traders and U.S. soldiers for purchases from natives.[151]

Cigarettes

Once smoking of cigarettes became widespread, they began to be used as currency. Like a coinage system, the single cigarette was excellent small change, and the pack of 20 and carton of 200 were quasi-decimal multiples. Best of all: they were nearly impossible to counterfeit.[152]

During and after World War II, cigarettes became a universal medium of exchange throughout Europe and Asia.[153] Prisoners of war, of course, had little choice, and rations from their captors and the Red Cross assured a steady supply even as many were smoked. In one camp, a British POW set up a stall, selling tea, coffee, or cocoa at two cigarettes a cup, buying the raw materials at market prices and hiring labor—including, at one point, an accountant! But "after a period of great prosperity he overreached himself and failed disastrously for several hundred cigarettes."[154]

  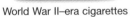 

World War II–era cigarettes

The Germans themselves, as well as residents of Austria, Italy, and the Netherlands, were little better off. Cigarettes were in such short supply that prices in terms of them were exceedingly low: in Vienna in 1947, an apartment could be rented for two packs per month.[155] Circulation in Thailand after the war was so widespread that prices in newspaper ads were quoted in cigarettes.[156]

Cigarette money returned in the 1980s in some dysfunctional Communist economies. It replaced distrusted local currency in Vietnam and Romania (different brands were demanded in each country, however); in Romania, smoking a cigarette was "like burning money."[157] In 1983, a pack of foreign cigarettes was "more valuable currency in Moscow's black markets than Soviet rubles [were] in the open market."[158]

Even now, in the United States, the use of cigarettes as money is widespread among prison inmates; they can be used to buy anything, from laundry service to sex.[159] And prohibition of smoking has only increased their purchasing power as contraband. At the Metropolitan Correctional Center in Chicago, a single cigarette was worth $10 in 2006, according to a prison official.[160]

Mind-Altering Drugs

The opium poppy has been grown for centuries in Southeast Asia. For the Wa people of Burma, opium was the chief crop, said to have been raised strictly for use as currency. In any case, in the 1990s poppy farmers did not use money, but bartered their opium directly for rice at a rate of 1 pound of opium for about 200 pounds of rice. In addition, the Wa collected taxes exclusively in opium, though foreign (Chinese) field owners used the Thai baht as currency.[161]

Opium poppy

In Argu, Afghanistan, a town near the Tajikistan border, local opium was an important barter item—if not actual money—for a time after the U.S. invasion. "Poppy farmers used opium as currency. They came to the Argu shops and exchanged their opium for wheat, for instance," said shopkeeper Haji Firouz in 2005. "Then the heroin makers came to the shops, bought the opium, gave us cash, and we would buy more goods for the shops."[162]

Cocaine

Though illegal, use of cocaine became so common in Hollywood among television producers, writers, and actors in the early 1980s that it became a form of money. "Cocaine is a negotiable instrument in this town," said one veteran producer, familiar with drug dealing. "You might not be able to pay a writer or an actor or director a bonus, so you pay him in cocaine." Several guest stars on a television variety show demanded more money than the designated "minimum" payment, so it was agreed that part of their fee would be paid in cocaine.[163]

OTHER NECESSITIES

Postage Stamps

Postage stamps have probably been used as money in some manner ever since their invention in 1840. Even now, they remain a convenient way to pay small debts by mail, and in the past they have seen much more extensive circulation during coin shortages.[164]

The earliest claimed use is from gold-rush California, though this has been disputed. The 25¢ local postage stamps of Adams & Co., San Francisco, were often used as currency because of the scarcity of coins, and supposedly, in 1854, a special printing of one stamp was made on Bristol board specifically for use as small change, it has been said.[165]

However, postage stamps certainly circulated east of the Rocky Mountains during the Civil War. By June 30, 1862, greenbacks fell to 92¢ in gold, and all silver coins vanished from circulation virtually overnight—leaving only the lowly cent in circulation. Postage stamps being the most universally accepted substitute for coins, the government actually made them essentially legal tender through an act signed by Abraham Lincoln on July 17, 1862: after August 1, they were receivable for government dues up to $5 and redeemable at all Treasury offices. Economist Neil Carothers later wrote: "It is at first glance difficult to believe that a responsible finance minister would propose the circulation of tiny squares of glue-coated paper as a national currency. Sheer panic is the only explanation of such a grotesque plan." Later in 1862, paper money replaced the unpopular stamps, which were then redeemed.[166]

Civil War–era U.S. postage stamps (actual size)

During and after World War I, postage stamps (including special printings on paper or cardboard) were pressed into currency use in Austria, Denmark, France, Germany, Great Britain, Greece, Japan, Korea, Madagascar, Russia, Serbia, South Russia, Taiwan, Turkey, and Ukraine. The Second World War saw similar usage in China, Cyprus, Great Britain, Guernsey, India, and Jersey.[167]

World War I Russian postage stamp with inscription on back for currency use (actual size)

Encased Stamps

During the U.S. Civil War, many people kept the stamps in little envelopes because of their flimsiness, and some envelopes with the value marked on the outside were specially printed for the purpose. But a better protection was the encasement, patented by John Gault of New York August 12, 1862. Gault's encasement consisted of a quarter-sized circular brass ring with a cover on one side, which held a slightly folded-over stamp beneath a mica window. On the reverse was an embossed brass disc with an advertisement for a business. Encased stamps were an instant success, despite costing buyers up to two cents over face value; the most popular were three, five, and 10 cents, which replaced hoarded silver coins, plus one cent. Encasements were used by 31 businesses in seven states and Canada over the next five months.[168]

Encased stamps returned in Europe after World War I, and the practice was revived in Shanghai in 1939 and in 1941 in Nazi-occupied Denmark.[169]

U.S. encased stamps (actual size)

Italian encased stamp (actual size)

1920 Danish encased stamp (actual size)

1941 Danish encased stamp (actual size)

4
ORNAMENTS

Among nomads and primitive peoples of all periods, wealth often took the form of ornaments. Our early ancestors wore beads; a dozen pierced mint-sized *Nassarius gibbosulus* shells, covered in red ochre and showing signs of being strung together, were excavated from Grotte des Pigeons, Taforalt, Morocco, in levels of circa 80,000 BC.[1] Two similar shell beads recovered in Israel were estimated to be 100,000 years old.[2] Ostrich eggshell beads from around 23,000 BC were found in Patne, Maharashtra, India.[3]

Materials to make these beads, and perhaps the beads themselves, were sometimes traded over long distances even during the Old Stone Age. At Yudinovo, Ukraine, archaeologists recovered beads and pendants made of marine shells dating from the very end of the Würm glacial period (about 12,000–8000 BC). The nearest source for these shells was almost 425 miles away.[4]

When ornaments were not only especially admired but also reasonably uniform, they became sufficiently fungible to pass into circulation as currency as well.

SHELL BEADS

Ostrich Eggshell Beads

A favorite currency among the Ovambo (or Owambo), Herero, and Bergdama tribes and the Nama (Khoikhoi) and San (Bushmen) peoples of Namibia until the early 20th century was so-called "bushmen's beads," discs cut out of ostrich eggshells, then soaked in water, pierced with an arrow point, and strung. Though used primarily as ornaments, they were also a medium of exchange in intertribal trade.[5]

Ostrich eggshell beads

Wampum and Other Indian Beads

In 1535, French explorer Jacques Cartier saw *esnurgny*, beads of white freshwater shells, among the Huron at Montreal; he later wrote that they had "the same use among them as gold and silver with us."[6]

True wampum, however, consisted of cylindrical shell beads about 1/4 of an inch long and 1/8 of an inch in diameter, used by the Iroquois circa 1570 to 1750. Normally it was white, but purple beads—cut from the heart of a clamshell—were also made, worth twice as much. Wampum was required for blood money; 20 strings of wampum 18 inches long would compensate for murder. It was also paid for ransoms and tribute.

The Dutch of New Netherland introduced wampum to New England in 1627, and it was legal tender, up to a shilling, in Massachusetts from 1637 to 1661. Wampum was used to pay the ferry fare between New York and Brooklyn as late as 1693, and unofficially passed as currency for many years thereafter.[7]

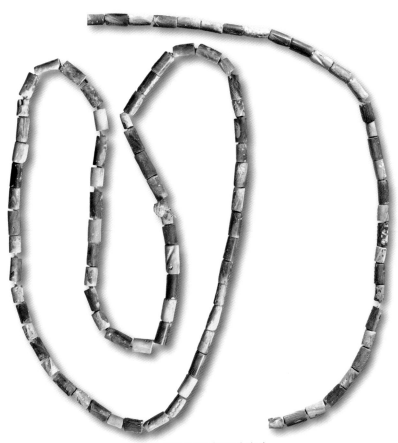

Wampum (actual size)

Rawrenock (called "roanoke" by the English), a string of discoidal clamshell beads, is mentioned as early as 1608 and was always described as money. First found on the Virginia and Carolina coasts, it circulated as late as the 18th century.[8]

Shell beads were an Indian currency on the West Coast as well. The Pomo and Chumash Indians of California used small, flat clamshell beads as money as late as 1926.[9]

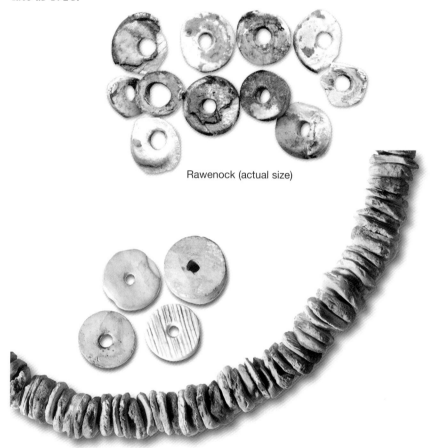

Rawenock (actual size)

Pomo Indian beads (actual size)

Sacred Shell Money of the Solomon Islands

In the southern Solomon Islands, marine shells were made into beautiful disk-shaped beads called *rongo*, meaning "sacred" in many Melanesian languages. They derived their value from the immense work that went into grinding and drilling them. One kind of seashell was used for white strings, *rongo pura*, and another for red strings, *rongo sisi;* a special kind was made from the very reddest part of the shell. Mixed strings were most common, though; red ones with patches of whites in the middle were called *sapi*.[10]

Rongo (actual size)

Early in the 20th century a lovesick Solomon Islander sang, "I broke off a long string of small shell beads and gave it to you, but you refused, therefore I am dissolved in tears. Surely your heart is longing for shell money." A man needed to accumulate or borrow many strings, as bride-price (circa 1880) was equal to 100 rongo sisi strings or 1,000 rongo pura strings. Rongo was also used for blood money payments and buying canoes. There was even special shell money for the use of women only, worth twice as much as standard money.[11]

Hippo Teeth Beads

Hippo teeth beads (actual size)

In West Africa, chiefly Nigeria and Ivory Coast, cattle were purchased in the 20th century with strings of "hippopotamus teeth"—but they were counterfeits, not real teeth at all, but *Arca* clamshell pendants from Singapore strung into necklaces.[12]

STONE AND CORAL BEADS
Mexican Jade Bead Money

No currency in pre-Columbian Mexico was more highly prized than jade. Aztec emperor Motecuhzoma Xocoyotzin assured Conquistador Bernal Díaz del Castillo that the finest jades were each worth two loads of gold, and jade was also current

Mexican jade beads
(actual size)

among the Mayas of Yucatan to purchase slaves and as grave offerings. Most Mexican jade money was in the form of thick beads varying from light gray to emerald green in color, about 1/2 inch in diameter.[13]

Magatama

Magatama (called *kogok* in Korea), pierced human embryo-shaped jewels carved from jade, agate, lapis lazuli, or carnelian, or made of colored glass, survive from the prehistory of Japan and Korea. Possibly intended to represent tiger claws, they date from circa 1000 BC to circa AD 794. They were clearly precious—large numbers have been found in graves and one is part of the Imperial Regalia of Japan—but in the absence of written records it is uncertain that they were actually used as money.

In both Japan and Korea, glass manufacturing seems to have been established for the sole purpose of making magatama. A magatama mold from circa 250 BC–AD 250 is the earliest evidence of glass production in Japan, and the Korean glass industry was founded during the Three Kingdoms period (57 BC–AD 668) for no other purpose.[14]

Magatama (actual size)

Tibetan Coral Beads

Marco Polo reported that the Tibetans "use no coined money, nor even the paper money of the Grand Khan, but for their currency employ coral [beads]." Polo added that Tibetan women wore necklaces of coral, "and with it ornament their idols."[15] In more recent times, all Tibetans donned large amounts of beads; the necklaces of noblewomen sometimes almost touched the ground.[16] Coral beads were used for purchases in Tibet into the 1960s.[17]

Tibetan coral beads (70% actual size)

CERAMIC BEADS

Donkey Beads

Donkey beads (actual size)

For centuries, locally-made, irregular blue faience beads strung on leather thongs have been tied to animals in Iran for protection against the evil eye. "Donkey beads" continue to be made in the holy city of Qom. They were sometimes used for small change.[18]

Udoud

Udoud encompasses the entire traditional money system of the Palau Islands of Micronesia, still essential for ceremonial gifts at major life events such as weddings, births, and funerals. Though only worn by women (and a new chief at his investiture ceremony), they are owned by men.[19]

Udoud (actual size)

The many varieties of beads comprising udoud arrived in Palau centuries ago under unknown circumstances, thought by the natives to be supernatural. They were already old in 1783 when first seen by a European; speculation as to their source has included Egypt, the Phoenicians, Japan, and the Portuguese, but the most probable include Cambay, India, or the Philippines, carried by Malay traders around 1600.[20] Whatever their origin, the total stock of udoud beads was frozen until 1990, though the beads admitted since then (equally old, from grave robbing in Indonesia and the Philippines) are rejected as counterfeit by elderly women of rank. Most pieces of udoud are so rare that each specimen has a name.[21]

The different types of beads were used for different purposes, from buying bananas or taro, making payments to sorcerers, or as a store of wealth by the very rich. Udoud was also lent at interest.[22] Freezing the stock of money prevented inflation and gradually gave each piece great value. Late in the 19th century a single bead could be worth up to 1,500 gold marks ($357), and in 2003, each genuine bead was worth between $100 and $100,000—though they are never sold to outsiders.[23]

Besides the porcelain beads, some types of udoud are made of glass or stone.[24]

GLASS TRADE BEADS

Chevron Beads

In the mid-1490s, Marietta Barovier, daughter of the famous Murano glassmaker Angelo Barovier, invented a colorful new kind of bead. Her large star or *rosetta* beads first appeared in Barovier's inventory in 1496; today they are known as chevron or paternoster beads.[25] The earliest examples, made up to circa 1610, have seven layers of glass, beginning at the core: transparent light blue-green, white, green again, white, red, white, and (usually) cobalt blue. Later chevron beads, including copies made in Amsterdam and Bohemia, have just six layers, omitting the innermost layer. (Beads with fewer layers and different colors were also made.) Since they were made in corrugated molds, when the bead was beveled at the end or rounded, the inner layers appeared as chevrons.[26]

Chevron beads were traded to native societies all over the world. Examples from pre-1550 sites were excavated in Florida, Peru, and Indonesia, and they continue to be very popular in Africa. In Sarawak, their name is *kelam batang umar*, "bead worth part of a house."[27]

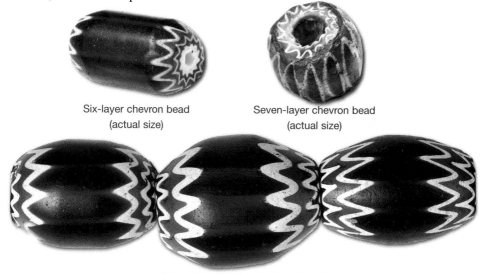

Six-layer chevron bead
(actual size)

Seven-layer chevron bead
(actual size)

String of chevron beads (actual size)

Cornaline d'Aleppo Beads

Another important Venetian trade bead was the *cornaline d'Aleppo* (carnelian of Aleppo), which imitated the carnelian gems from Syria thought to ward off diseases; they were later known as white heart or "Hudson's Bay beads." They had a brick-red outer surface (sometimes under clear glass) and a yellow, white, green, or other-colored core.[28]

Cornaline d'Aleppo
(actual size)

The Spanish traded them in Guatemala, perhaps as early as the 16th century. Early examples of these beads have been excavated at a Seneca site in western New York State dating to between circa 1630 and circa 1650, and later forms were found at other North American Indian settlements up to 1875; the Hudson's Bay Company exchanged six cornaline d'Aleppo beads for one "made beaver" as late as the 1920s. They were also traded into Africa during the 19th century in exchange for ivory and palm oil.[29]

Aggry Beads

When the Portuguese explorer Duarte Pacheco Pereira visited the Gold Coast about 1480, he saw "certain blue beads which they call *coris*" used in trade. By the early 17th century the name had become *accory*, as a result of the local Fante people adding a vowel to the beginning of any word starting with a consonant. Still later, g replaced c, giving us the modern name *aggry*. In the 15th century these beads were so valuable that the Portuguese used them to purchase gold.

Aggry bead
(actual size)

The true aggry was a tubular bead that appeared blue in daylight, but green in transmitted light. Though the Portuguese obtained them from Benin, they were probably exported to West Africa from Egypt.[30]

Millefiori Beads

Colorful Venetian *millefiori* (thousand flowers) beads were exported to West Africa along the Gulf of Guinea, where they substituted for the rare aggry beads, and to Indonesia. Their dating is uncertain; millefiori beads were apparently made in small quantities before 1800, but the majority date from circa 1825 to 1900.[31]

Millefiori glass is covered with a repetitive pattern of starry or flowerlike designs. It was made by arranging a bundle of colored glass rods so that its end resembled the design wanted. Subjected to intense heat, the bundle was fused into a single rod or cane. While still in a plastic state it was then pulled to a great length; the original design was preserved—but shrunken to miniature size. Construction of a bead was done by fusing slices of the canes together, sometimes using a dark matrix glass around them or employing a mold.[32]

Millefiori beads (actual size)

While millefiori beads were very valuable and were used for bride-price along the Gold Coast, they do not seem to have been a medium of exchange there, though along the Liberian coast the Kru people considered each bead equal to one Spanish dollar.[33]

"Padre" Beads

In 1565, the Spanish began transshipping Chinese goods via Manila to Acapulco on the west coast of Mexico. Missionaries to the Pima and Papago Indians of Arizona thus acquired satin-finish, opaque, sky-blue Chinese glass beads about 3/8 of an inch in diameter, and these are consequently known as "padre" or "chief" beads. Imports apparently stopped in the 18th century, making padre beads rare heirlooms: in 1900 the Pimas would sell a good horse for 30 padre beads, and they continued to prize them as recently as 1971.[34]

Padre beads (50% actual size)

Very similar beads were traded to the Indians of the Northwest in the 18th and 19th centuries, including white beads and other sizes, and copies are also found among African beads.[35]

"Russian" Beads

Russian beads (actual size)

Starting in the latter part of the 18th century, traders in Russian America (Alaska) bought furs with multifaceted short glass beads of translucent deep ultramarine blue; unopened packages of them remained behind in Sitka after the U.S. purchase in 1867. Beads of this type, with about 18 to 24 facets (sometimes many more) and about 1/4 to 3/4 of an inch in diameter, have since been known as "Russian" beads, though they are thought to have been made in Bohemia.[36]

Russian beads were one of the most widely distributed Indian trade beads. They were used in trade in the western Great Lakes area from about 1760 to 1820 and in the American Southwest from circa 1775 to circa 1850, and in other areas from 1820 into the 1840s. Along the Northwest coast, Columbia River Indians would sell a beaver or three martins for six to eight beads.[37]

Similar hexagonal blue beads, but lacking the facets, were traded in Africa from the 1860s to about 1900, in some cases used to buy slaves.[38]

"Trade Wind" (Indo-Pacific) Beads

From circa 250 BC to AD 1600, the port of Arikamedu on the southeast coast of India was a major center of glass bead production, its products appearing from Africa to Korea. Later, similar beads were made by Indian glassmakers throughout Southeast Asia. Perhaps the greatest trade beads of all time, they have been called "trade wind" beads because they were carried by merchants sailing the monsoon winds, though "Indo-Pacific" beads better describes their centers of production. Similar beads are still made in the area.[39]

True Indo-Pacific beads are small, shiny, monochrome, rounded drawn-glass beads of seed bead size or a little larger, suitable for sewing on garments,

Trade wind beads (actual size)

though some were worn as necklaces; larger sizes appear to have been made more recently. The most common colors are brick red, yellow, turquoise, green, and blackish-blue.[40]

Trade wind beads reached East Africa as early as AD 200, where they served as small change, and they were plentiful in South Africa from 1000 to 1250. Caravans took them across the Sahara desert into Ghana.[41] In the Kingdom of Monomotapa (modern-day Zimbabwe), Muslim traders used them to buy gold.[42] A little later, Indo-Pacific beads were used as currency in the Swahili towns of the East African coast.[43]

Nearly two-thirds of the beads used in the Philippines from about AD 1 through circa 1200 were Indo-Pacific beads, and the brick red beads were treasured as heirlooms in Timor and other parts of Indonesia, where they were called *mutisalah*. In 1965, a 12-inch-long string would purchase a water buffalo there.[44]

Rings of All Kinds

Rings have served the dual functions of jewelry and money since ancient times, since they offer security against loss. One formed part of the bride-price of Rebekah: "the man took a golden [nose] ring of half a shekel weight, and two bracelets for her hands of ten shekels weight of gold" (Gen. 24:22). Later, to restore the wealth of Job, "every man also gave [Job] a *qesitah* [piece of money], and every one [a] ring of gold" (Job 42:11).

Gold Rings

Small, open gold rings of many forms, dating to the late Bronze Age (circa 1150–750 BC), are found throughout Britain and Ireland. Once assumed to be ring money, Colin McEwan of the Department of Ethnography of the British Museum now thinks them to be personal adornment of some sort—perhaps hair or nose rings—though as portable wealth they may well have served as media of exchange in those prehistoric times.[45] Similar rings are known from the Middle East.[46]

Gold ring money (50% actual size)

Silver Jewelry

After 1868, Navajo smiths began making articles from silver dollars, and shortly afterwards, setting them with turquoise. Such jewelry is highly valued by Navajos and never depreciates, making it both a standard of deferred payment and a store of value. Like modern "hard asset" investors, Navajos buy jewelry with their cash earnings surplus. They then pawn it as needed to purchase supplies, redeeming it when wool or lambs are sold.[47]

Navajo silver jewelry

Torcs and Neck Rings

Torcs—elaborate circular neck rings, usually of solid, twisted gold, silver, or bronze—were all the fashion in late Iron Age Europe. Those of gold are sometimes found in hoards, such as in Snettisham, England, where scores of torcs were buried circa 75 BC in a dozen deposits, though it is thought that all this wealth was hidden for ritual purposes and not simply for concealment. The "Great Torc" in one of these hoards contained over 1 kilogram of gold.[48]

Snettisham hoard of British torcs

Several hill tribes of Thailand, Vietnam, and Laos (chiefly the Hmong or Méo) make silver neck rings and bracelets, solid, hollow, and twisted. Adventurer Harry Franck, who visited the Méo in 1926, wrote: "Another custom of these sturdy mountaineers is the wearing about their necks of heavy silver rings of all shapes. These are evidently concerned with their tribal superstitions as well as being their idea of combining adornment with safe banking. All silver money that falls in their hands is turned into rings; men, women, even the children, all wear them. . . . The richest of them clanked like perambulating pawnshops whenever they moved."[49]

Hmong neck rings (25% actual size)

Yoruba neck rings (25% actual size)

Neck rings of copper and brass—though far heavier than those of gold or silver—also had a monetary function in sub-Saharan Africa in the 19th and 20th centuries. These massive collars, reportedly weighing up to 33 pounds, became a kind of currency for bride-price and payments for livestock, food, services, and fines in the 19th century among some Congo tribes and the Yoruba of Nigeria. Those of the Congo were so valuable, yet so difficult to take off, that a woman captured by enemies risked being decapitated.[50]

Arm Rings and Bracelets

Shell arm rings were an important currency throughout Melanesia, from the Torres Straits to the Solomon Islands. Though the shells were common, manufacture was restricted to only a few centers, where the men were thought to have the necessary magic.

In the islands south of New Guinea, *Conus* shell armlets called *wauri* morphed from ornaments to money by the early 20th century; a wauri would buy a canoe, a harpoon, or a wife. The shell of the giant clam, *Tridacna gigas*, was used in New

Poata armlet (75% actual size)

Guinea proper and the islands to the east of New Ireland. A well-decorated arm ring *(poata)* would buy at least 300 pounds of sago. In New Britain, thin, fluted arm rings had even greater purchasing power: 500 pounds of sago, as of 1935. They were also essential for bride-price; in the Solomon Islands, a girl sang to her lover, "Buy me with arm rings. . . ."[51]

Copper and brass armlets and bracelets were preferred in Africa. Late in the 17th century brass arm rings *(bochie)* were currency in southern Nigeria, with brass and iron bracelets used as late as the 20th century.[52]

Bochie (75% actual size)

Leg Rings and Anklets

Native copper from sources to the north of the Congo basin was worked into huge ornaments for trade and currency: one Ngombe anklet weighs nearly 5 pounds. Other heavy leg rings were used as currency throughout West Africa as late as the 1980s.[53]

African anklets

SHELLS

Cowry Shells

While shells have been traded since the Stone Age, one type in particular has attained almost universal monetary status: the money cowry, *Cypraea Moneta*, used as money for millennia. Convenient in size and with a naturally polished, white porcelain appearance, cowries were also prized at times as fertility symbols (from their resemblance to the vulva) and as protection against the evil eye (from their oval shape). Cypraea Moneta is found from the Indian Ocean to as far east as the Galapagos Islands, but was chiefly collected in the Maldive Islands. "Cowry" is derived from the Hindi and Urdu *kauri*.[54]

Modern cowry
shells (actual size)

Cowries were introduced into China in the Neolithic period and became a medium of exchange during the Shang Dynasty, about the 16th century BC. They began to be used as money around the beginning of the succeeding Zhou Dynasty, circa 1122 BC. Imitations were even made of shell, bone, wood, ceramic, and metal.[55] The Chinese character *huò*, meaning goods, is formed from the characters for spend (*huā*) and cowry (*bèi*).[56] In 852 BC, cowries and tortoise shells were brought in from south China for monetary purposes.[57]

Chinese Shang
Dynasty cowries
(actual size)

Chinese imitation
cowries (actual size)

Many cowries found in China have had their backs broken for stringing. They were banned as currency in China in 221 BC, save for a brief revival under the emperor Wang Mang in AD 10. However, they remained the principal money of Yunnan in south China as late as the 13th century.[58]

Elsewhere in Asia, cowries circulated from India to Indochina, and were used as small change in Benares, Darjeeling, and Hyderabad bazaars into the first half of the 20th century.[59]

Cowries were also highly desired in Africa from at least the 14th century. When first introduced into Uganda about 1800, two shells would purchase a woman—but within two generations, so many had been imported that a woman could scarcely be bought for 10,000 cowries.[60] They were acceptable for tax payments there until 1901.[61] In Nigeria cowries were generally strung, but for large payments they were packed in sacks; especially large quantities were sewn into mats of 20,000 cowries each. They were still used as money in some markets as late as 1955.[62]

Though cowries are common in Oceania, they were seldom used for money outside of the interior of Papua New Guinea. But there they were avidly sought; in 1924, a woman could be purchased for 10 cowries and a piglet for as few as two. Here again, large imports lowered their value so much that by 1936 the bride-price was at least a nine-foot length of cowries, sewn on cord. As late as 1943, trails and airstrips were constructed in the interior of New Guinea with the aid of natives who would take no other form of money but cowries.[63]

Broken-back cowries (above: 55% actual size; right: 85% actual size)

Dentalium Shells

Dentalium shells (90% actual size)

Tusk-shaped *Dentalium pretiosum* shells were the principal money of West Coast North American Indian tribes from northern California to Alaska. The longer the shell, the greater its value: among the Yuroks of California, a shell 2-1/2 inches long was worth 20 times as much as one just 5/8 of an inch shorter. If only 1-1/2 inches long, it was good only for small change; shorter ones were worthless. The Yurok monetary unit was a string of 27-1/2 inches.[64] Farther north, the unit was a fathom: the Chinook standard was 40 shells, but if 39 made a fathom, it was worth double.[65] Among the Nootka Indians of Alaska, 5 fathoms would purchase a slave.[66] Dentalium shells circulated from before 1800 to the 1920s.[67]

Pearl Shells

Throughout much of Micronesia, beautiful pearl shells were used as money to pay for building a house or canoe until well into the 20th century. On Kusaie in the Caroline Islands, pieces cut from these shells formed the currency and the larger the shell, the higher the value. On Yap, pearl shells were considered exclusively women's money, being used (among other things) for bride-price and payments to village prostitutes. They were ground at the edge and strung on cords.[68]

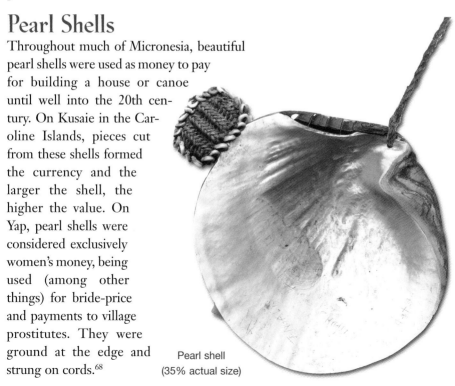

Pearl shell
(35% actual size)

Kina Shells

The gold lip shell, locally called *kina*, was the favored currency of Papua New Guinea for bride-price payments from about 1800 to 1985. These large shells were pierced twice and worn around the neck. Kina was legal tender as late as the 1960s at the rate of 12 shillings per pair.[69]

Kina shell (50% actual size)

TEETH

Dog and Porpoise Teeth

A single dog's tooth could buy 100 coconuts in the Solomon Islands at one time, but later only 10 in the Admiralty Islands. Generally just the canine teeth were used, either in groups of four or up to 100 strung on a necklace. They also circulated in New Guinea between about 1850 and 1960, where the numbering system was based on them (4 = a dog, 8 = 2 dogs, etc.). Prior to the 1930s, German traders introduced counterfeits made of porcelain.[70]

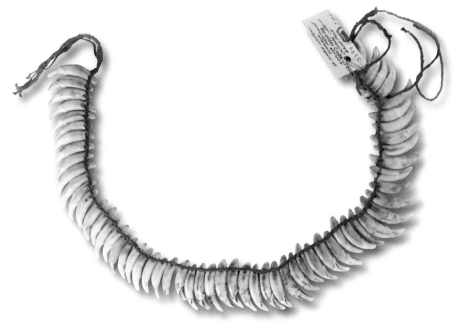

Dog teeth (40% actual size)

Porpoise teeth were also money in the Solomons, at a rate of five porpoise teeth to a dog's tooth as of 1883. They are still used for bride-price, at a minimum of 1,000 teeth per healthy wife.[71]

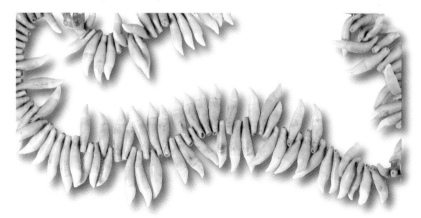

Porpoise teeth (45% actual size)

Boar's Tusks

Wild boar's tusks were highly prized currency in New Guinea and New Hebrides—but only when grown into a full circle. Natives knocked out the two incisor teeth in the upper jaw, permitting the lower tusks to grow unimpeded, finally piercing the lower jaw bone. Such tusks were worth 200 dog's teeth around 1900, and are still used for bride-price.[72]

Full circle boar's tusk (95% actual size)

Whale's Teeth

On Fiji, *tambua* (sperm whale's teeth strung on cords, though originally made of wood) were hoarded as wealth and used in exchanges. A single tooth could buy a big canoe, and was essential as a betrothal gift from the 1840s into the 1940s.[73]

Whale tooth (45% actual size)

BONES

"Flying Fox" Jaws

Fruit-eating bats of the genus *Pteropus* are the world's largest bats, so big that they are commonly known as flying foxes. Quick and nocturnal, they are hard to catch, so they have a scarcity value. While their teeth alone have been used as currency in New Ireland and the Solomon Islands, the entire lower jaw also circulated in Fiji in the 1880s, singly or on strings, sometimes blackened with tar.[74]

"Flying fox" jaws (actual size)

Shark Vertebrae

Like shell beads, strings of shark vertebrae—which have a natural central hole—circulated in parts of Melanesia and Polynesia in the 19th and 20th centuries, particularly in the Society Islands.[75]

Shark vertebrae (actual size)

FEATHERS

Late in the 19th century, natives of the Southern Banks Islands (now part of Torba Province, Vanuatu) made *wetapup* by binding the little feathers near the eyes of fowls, sometimes dyed a beautiful crimson, on strings. Wetapup was used as necklaces and anklets, and also passed as money. (By the mid-20th century, longer and coarser feathers were used, and some were bound on sticks.) Elsewhere in Melanesia, cassowary feathers and bird of paradise plumes were part of the bride-price in New Guinea early in the 20th century.[76]

Feather sticks (60% actual size)

CUSTOMARY OBJECTS

NONWEARABLE RINGS

Shell and Stone

Quantities of polished seashell rings about an inch in diameter have been found in inland Syria in graves dating between 3500 and 3000 BC and were possibly used as currency in ancient Mesopotamia.[1] Rings made of the shell of the giant clam were certainly money in 18th- through 20th-century Melanesia, however. Among many locations involved was Nissan Island, east of New Ireland, where rough, heavy rings unsuitable for use as ornaments were made for trade with the mainland.[2]

Turtle shell was prized throughout Oceania, and turtle shell rings and disks were considered money on several islands, particularly the Northern Mariana Islands, Guam, and Yap.[3]

Stone rings, called *navela*, were the most precious heirlooms on Vanuatu early in the 20th century and were believed not to be made by human hands. The largest rings weighed up to 50 pounds each, and were so huge that a man could easily crawl through the center, while others were small enough to be buried in the ground. This money

Ancient shell rings
(actual size)

Giant clam ring (25% actual size)

Turtle shell rings (50% actual size)

was absolutely theft-proof, since each navela was recognizable by sight, and had its own name and history. Navela were chiefly used as wife-buying money and as presents at feasts.[4]

Lead, Potin, and Bronze

Small knobbed rings or spoked wheels of lead or potin (a grayish alloy of high-tin bronze) are thought to have been used as currency in ancient Gaul. Similar bronze rings, sometimes knobbed but usually smooth, have been attributed as "Celtic" ring money and dated to the 11th to the first century BC. While large quantities are found from the eastern Balkans north to Bohemia, and as far west as England—all areas of Celtic settlement—not only their monetary use but even their date has been doubted.[5] Those from Moravia occur in at least five "denominations."[6] The Swiss Lake Dwellers made large bronze rings from which smaller ones were suspended, often in pairs of fixed weights.[7]

Celtic ring money (actual size)

Celtic ring money (55% actual size)

In the 1880s, archaeologist Jacques de Morgan excavated many plain bronze rings a few inches across from ancient tombs in northern Armenia, made apparently to standard weights. Since the best-furnished tombs had the most rings, de Morgan concluded that they were "actual money comprising the fortune of the person buried in the tomb," though this was doubted by later scholars.[8]

The Kadman Numismatic Museum in Tel Aviv has on display several sizes of bronze rings thought to have been used as money in ancient Israel. About 25 bronze rings dating from circa 1200 to circa 1000 BC, in two or three sizes ranging from 2 to 3-3/4 inches in diameter, were found together in Jerusalem about 1980.[9]

Manillas

For more than 500 years manillas were an important form of money over much of the forest areas of West Africa from Sénégal to Cameroon. The name "manilla," meaning bracelet, is seemingly of Iberian origin, but its form—an open bracelet with flared ends—is African.[10]

Manillas (actual size)

From the mid-10th century, rods of copper suitable for making bracelets were traded south across the Sahara desert for gold.[11] The first true manillas, though, were ordered from Venice for this trade by Portugal in 1439.[12] Later in that century, Portugal reached West Africa by sea, greatly increasing its African trade; it purchased 450,000 manillas in 1498 from Flanders, and also introduced manillas of brass.[13]

Manillas were used to buy slaves along the West African coast, especially in the kingdom of Benin, where they were mostly melted to cast decorative plaques for the *Oba*'s palaces. These plaques show that by then, manillas were purely objects of value, not bracelets. At

Benin plaque showing manillas
(15% actual size)

first slaves cost only a few manillas, but after 1500 the price rose to as much as 57 manillas; pepper, gold, and ivory were also purchased and experienced a similar inflation. The depreciation of the manilla was caused by the hundreds of thousands imported in the early 16th century.[14]

Dutch, Castilian, and Danish traders also sent manillas to Africa in the 15th through 17th centuries. One German offered manillas of such bad quality in 1603 that the natives threatened to eat him![15] From the mid-17th century, the French bought ivory with manillas in Senegal, Sierra Leone, and the Ivory Coast. Late in the 19th century they traded copper-lead manillas to the Congo basin, and manillas were used to buy palm oil at Grand-Bassam, Ivory Coast, until the 20th century.[16] They circulated in parts of French West Africa well into the 1950s.[17]

The English entered the African trade about 1550, trading manillas for ivory, pepper, and gold.[18] Tin manillas were made for Gambia before 1668, and lead was added to copper manillas beginning in the late 1720s; later British manillas contained more than 30 percent lead. By 1836 production had passed firmly to Birmingham, and while the alloy was more or less constant, a bewildering variety of patterns began to be produced.[19] Twenty years later five patterns were in use in Nigeria, all very similar, yet natives could discriminate between them at once. One type was good at all markets, but the others only at certain places, and one was worth only half as much as the rest.[20]

Nigerians were serious about using the right manilla. If someone refused to accept the pattern required at the local market, he could be killed; around 1905, one fellow made the mistake of rejecting the manillas current in the Ohambele market; he found himself tied to a stake next to the market *juju* as a sacrifice and left to die of thirst.[21]

Nigeria banned import of manillas in 1902, though they remained legal tender until 1911. They continued to circulate in remote villages, however, where they were required to buy palm oil. Native middlemen converted sterling to manillas for the native palm oil buyers, and manillas back to sterling for tax payments, but this system led to abuses. It was decided to redeem all Nigerian manillas by March 31, 1949, after which use would be prohibited. The premium paid was so high that many people dug up their savings and even stole manillas thrown away as sacrifices to gods. Over 32 million manillas were surrendered and scrapped.[22]

Yet one Nigerian complained that this action was nothing short of robbery, asserting that his grandfather "lost

Nigerian manilla (actual size)

King manilla (40% actual size)

his fortune" (in manillas) when they were demonetized. And it is true that the price of a bride or of food—expressed in manillas—was constant for long periods, unlike for later paper money.[23]

Beginning in the 19th century, giant manillas were made by native smiths in several sizes ("king," "queen," and "prince") as high values and symbols of wealth; they were used for dowries and funerals.[24]

Gold

The Egyptians used gold ring money in the period before the Exodus, as we know from tomb paintings of the 15th and 14th centuries BC showing doughnuts of gold being weighed on enormous scales, balanced against animal-shaped weights. The units were the *deben* (seven *deben* equaled about 3 troy ounces) and the kite (1/10 of a *deben*).[25]

Painting from the tomb of Benia (10% actual size)

More recently, gold rings were used as money in northern Sudan in the 19th and early 20th centuries. In the 1830s, traveler Robert Curzon encountered a curious vessel at Aswan, below the First Cataract, sailing north to Cairo from Sudan. The captain, a European, showed Curzon "three or four strongly-made iron-bound chests, which, on being opened, proved to be full of gold, to the amount of some thousands of pounds . . . most part of it was in rings the size of bracelets, and others the size of large, heavy finger-rings, all of pure gold. These rings were passed as money."[26]

Ethiopian gold ring
(actual size)

To the south and east of Sudan, gold rings circulated in Ethiopia also in the 19th and 20th centuries. In 1901 according to French writer and traveler Hugues Le Roux, native gold washers sold their dust and nuggets to a broker, "who works it into circles of pure gold of about the thickness of a heavy finger ring. These circles are not closed, so that the buyer may twist them before weighing, thus assuring himself, upon finding them malleable, that no copper has been mixed with the pure metal." The gold rings were exchangeable for silver by weight at a rate of 1:31, paid in Maria Theresia thalers.[27]

TRADITIONAL SILVER FORMS

Larins

Shortly after 1500, the king of Lar, a city in southern Iran near the Persian Gulf, began taking long pieces of thick silver wire, bending them double, and stamping

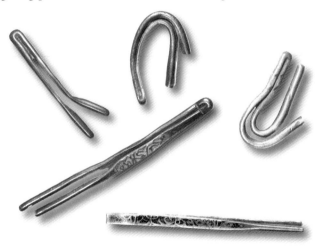

Larins (actual size)

them with dies. These so-called *larins* quickly became the standard trade money throughout Persia and western India as far south as the Maldive Islands and Sri Lanka.[28] Persian larins were replaced by coins by 1666, but they continued to be made in India until 1672.[29] In Ceylon and the Maldive Islands they were bent into a fishhook shape, and private copies continued to be made as late as 1800. Base silver larins, called *toweelah*, were issued in al-Hasa province, Arabia, from circa 1703 to circa 1775, and copper and pewter ones were minted in Java, circa 1658.[30]

Siamese Bullet Money

Open silver bracelets bearing notches and stamps were used as money in ancient Thailand, apparently evolving into a crescent shape too small to wear. Perhaps as early as the 11th century, miniature pieces were made with the ends hammered together. Gradually they became thicker and rounder, eventually resembling spherical bullets. They were the principal money of Siam until 1860, and were legal tender to 1904.[31]

1/16 through 1 baht
Siamese bullet money
(actual size)

Eighteen denominations were coined in silver, plus a further nine in gold. However, the most common were the *baht* and its half (2 *salu'ng*), quarter (*salu'ng*), eighth (*fuang*), and sixteenth (*sik*). Later pieces were made by scoring a bar, placing it in a depression, rounding it with five blows, and applying appropriate dynastic and royal stamps.[32]

K'a K'im

K'a k'im (actual size)

Even odder than bullet money is the *k'a k'im* of Northern Thailand. These curious rings—split and bent into the shape of a woman's pelvis—were used as money circa 1325 to 1545. They are stamped with a denomination, dynasty symbol, and name of the mint city.[33]

Tiger Tongues (*Lat*)

Circa 1353 to 1889, silver and copper alloy ingots called *lat* were the money of the Mekong Valley from Xishuangbanna in southern Yunnan down to the Cambodian

Tiger tongues (actual size)

border, including parts of modern Laos and Thailand. From their shape, various lat have been nicknamed leech or canoe money; those with lines of bumps were called tiger tongues.[34]

Toks

Toks, clamshell-shaped silver ingots, were used in northern Thailand and Burma until 1871. Those of Chiang Mai, called pig's-mouth money, are heavily domed, while those of Nan—larger than a silver dollar, but debased—are flatter. Shan toks are smaller. Chiang Mai and Nan toks have a yellowish deposit on one side that is said to come from pouring the molten metal on egg yolk, though it is apparently caused by impurities.[35]

Chaing Mai, Nan, and Shan toks (actual size)

TRADITIONAL BASE METAL FORMS

Four-Armed Copper Ingots

As early as the eighth century AD, copper miners in Central Africa began casting H-shaped ingots for trade. There was considerable size variation at first, but
by circa 1400 two well-defined types of currency had developed. In southeastern
Congo, they were more cross-like and ranged in length from 1/4 of an inch to
over 6 inches, but in the Zambia-Zimbabwe area they had long arms, a flange on
the bottom edge, and weighed around 8 pounds. Similar ingots were cast at
Great Zimbabwe. Smaller H-shaped crosses from Sanga, in eastern Katanga near
Lake Tanganyika, are mostly later, made until the 18th century.[36]

H-shaped copper ingots (actual size)

Later, huge X-shaped "Katanga crosses" were cast, typically in sand molds made by the miner's fingers. About 9 inches across and usually weighing somewhat more than 2 pounds, they were the principal money of Katanga from the mid-18th century to the 1920s, and were never refused as payment. Five or six crosses would purchase a wife in Lualaba prior to 1924. A local magistrate, upon finding a pile of crosses, some pieces of cloth, and a pair of suspenders on his desk in the 1920s, exclaimed, "Hullo, a dowry returned. Another divorce."[37]

Katanga cross (60% actual size)

Brass Rods and Copper Trolley Wire

Copper and brass rods were used as money throughout West and Central Africa from the 12th century into the 20th century, accepted in payment for all kinds of goods from eggs to slaves. Traders, travelers, and missionaries frequently brought coils of wire, including worn-out copper trolley wire, from which pieces were cut off as needed.[38]

About 1/4 of an inch in diameter, brass rods varied in length with place and time. And "coin clipping" was a problem: missionary W.H. Bentley wrote, "In 1894 we noticed that a large number of rods in the Church Treasury Box were more than twice the length of those then current; we therefore cut them down to the current length of 10 inches and sold the little pieces to local blacksmiths. By keeping the rods, their value had more than doubled."[39] Or had it? As the rods grew shorter, prices rose, with the price of a fowl increasing from two or three rods to 150 over a 30-year period. In Joseph Conrad's novella *Heart of Darkness* (based on his experiences in the Congo in 1890), the native steamer crew was "given . . . every week three pieces of brass wire, each about nine inches long; and the theory was they were to buy their provisions with that currency in river-side villages."[40]

Brass rod
(15% actual size)

U-shaped Rods

Boloko
(15% actual size)

U-shaped copper rods with splayed feet (*boloko*) were a favorite currency in the Congo from around 1900 to 1950; one boloko would buy a he-goat, three a female slave, and 10 boloko a wife.[41]

"Ant-Nose" or "Ghost Head" Money

The money of the ancient Chinese State of Chu included small bronze replicas of cowry shells, pierced at one end for stringing. At least nine different inscriptions are known on these "coins"; their meaning is unclear, though some may be denominations. From their appearance, they were called *yǐ bí qián*, "ant-nose copper coin," or *guǐ tóu*, "ghost head" money. Though traditionally ant-nose money was introduced by Sunshu Ao, Prime Minister of Zhuang, Duke of Chu (613–591 BC), it is now dated to the Warring States Period, between circa 475 and 223 BC.[42]

"Ant-nose" money
(2x actual size)

"Fish" and "Bridge" Money

"Fish" money (50% actual size)

"Bridge" money (50% actual size)

Hoards of uninscribed but holed bronze objects shaped like fish or bridges have been found in China and are thought by some to have been used as money circa 700 BC. The bridge-shaped pieces are attributed to the State of Chu.[43]

Tin Fish and Cocks

From the 15th to the 19th centuries, Malayan tin miners cast ingots in the form of animals *(gambar)* as well as in plain blocks. These passed as money by weight.

Among the gambar types were fish, cock, crocodile, tortoise, elephant, goat, locust, and mantis, all of definite weight. The sum of 2-1/2 cents was still nicknamed a "crocodile" in the coastal districts of Selangor as late as 1906.[44]

Tin animals (35% actual size)

Tin Hat Ingots

Other Malayan tin money resembles square hats. In the Pahang Sultanate, tin miners favored casting the *tampang* (tin ingot) in the shape of a truncated pyramid, since it was easy to withdraw from the mold. Over time, a square plinth was added, and finally the plinth became wider and the pyramid smaller and hollow—giving rise to a "tin hat" shape. These hollow ingots could be nested for convenience and, with the addition of a hole for stringing, were very suitable for currency.[45]

They were issued in four sizes, valued at one, one-half, one-quarter, and one-eighth tampang, and bear dates from 1235 to 1295 (AD 1819–1878). In 1890, a Pahang Sultanate tampang was worth 4¢. Tin hat money was demonetized in 1893.[46]

Tin hat ingots (50% actual size)

Mamuli

Since the early 19th century, an essential part of bride-price in Sumba, Indonesia, is *mamuli*—jewels representing stylized female genitalia, given by the groom's family. Notwithstanding their shape, those with "feet" (flaring bases, usually ornamented with miniature figures of men or animals) are considered male, while those with less flared, plainer bases are female. When the

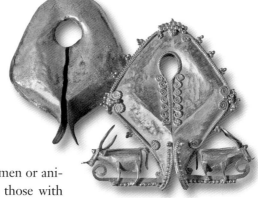

Mamuli (75% actual size)

Sumbanese practiced artificial earlobe elongation, mamuli were worn as earrings; later they became pendants or bangles. Mamuli range from plain, tin-plated copper pieces to elaborately-ornamented jewels of silver and even gold.[47]

Drums (Mokos)

Huge bronze kettledrums or gongs (*mokos*) were the most highly valued money of Alor Island, Indonesia. Hourglass-shaped and richly decorated, generally with four handles, they were originally made of bronze, though thousands of brass mokos were imported about 1900.[48] These drums originated in the Dông So'n culture of northern Vietnam between circa 1500 and 500 BC; examples are found throughout Southeast Asia. But it was only much later on Alor that they turned into money.[49]

Only damaged mokos actually circulated, as perfect ones were kept for ceremonial purposes. There were 19 "denominations" of mokos, with various values: a single *piki moko* purchased a pig (worth about five rupiahs) around 1940, while an *itkira moko* was valued at up to 3,000 rupiahs. Mokos were an indispensable component of bride-price.[50] Lending and borrowing mokos kept the men of Alor so busy that they had no time for gardening or physical labor, which was done by women.[51]

The Dutch colonial government attempted to abolish the moko system in 1914, when it banned their import and had 1,600 that were turned in for tax payments crushed and melted. However, the Alorese held many back. Mokos are used for purchase of brides even now.[52]

Moko (30% actual size)

"God Bells" (Deoganta)

In 1879, the Hill Miri tribe of Lakhimpur, India, south of Tibet, sometimes used Tibetan "god bells" (*deoganta*) as money, valuing them at from one-quarter to 12 rupees, depending on shape, size, and decoration.[53]

Deoganta
(40% actual size)

AFRICAN IRON MONEY

Iron smelting penetrated virtually all of Africa by the end of the sixth century AD.[54] Besides weapons and tools, bracelets and other jewelry were made from iron. These objects could be traded within each tribe, or to neighboring tribes lacking good ores and smelters. In time, trading goods evolved which were not useful in and of themselves, but were recognizable as uniform and made from good iron. They thus became media of exchange, standards of value, and (since wrought iron resists rusting) stores of value—in short, money.[55]

Throwing-Knife

One exotic currency of the Congo and other parts of north-central Africa was the throwing-knife. While round knives are known, they are usually shaped more or less like a letter F, Z, Y, E, or I, augmented by a bewildering variety of hooks, spikes, discs, and other shapes; over 200 varieties are known.[56]

Throwing-knife money derived its value from custom, not its utility as a weapon, as some have blades too thin to be useful and most were never actually thrown. In fact, if they were thrown and then lost, the owner would literally be "throwing his money away." About 1900, *shongo*, the throwing-knife currency of the Kasai and Sankuru river area, was worth "a hundred times" its value as metal, and a single knife could purchase several slaves.[57]

Throwing-knife money
(15% actual size)

Liganda

In the 19th and early 20th centuries, Congo blacksmiths made giant spearheads, some taller than a man. These were used as money by the Lokele, Turumbu, Budja, Topoke, and neighboring peoples. This currency was called *liganda* or *ngbele*.[58]

The smiths started with two sheets of iron, which they soldered together. After shaping, they made a series of incisions with a chisel along the entire length of each side parallel to the edge, and then added a cylindrical extension for a wooden shaft, so that the currency could be driven into the ground.[59]

The longer the spear, the more valuable it was. There were two or three denominations of liganda: the huge *doa*, between about 5 feet 8 inches and 6 feet 6 inches high by about 15 inches wide; the *dihunga*, approximately 5 feet by 9 inches, of which three were roughly equal to one doa; and an intermediate size, thought to be worth two dihunga. Despite their great length, liganda weigh only about 4 to 5 pounds each.

This impressive currency had high purchasing power. Between 1907 and 1922, 30 doa could buy a male slave, and for 40 to 50, a free woman could be bought as a wife. Though no longer made, as late as 1949 they were still used to purchase canoes and for bride-price payments.[60]

Liganda (7.5% actual size)

"Kissi Penny" (*Kilindi*)

Of all African iron money, the most famous is the *kilindi* or "Kissi penny" of West Africa. For 200 years the Kissi tribe has dwelled mostly in small villages in forest clearings in Guinea, Liberia, and Sierra Leone, near the area where the three countries meet. Western visitors usually describe them as primitive, and nearly 90 percent practice their traditional religion.

Sometime between about 1860 and 1900 Kissi blacksmiths began making long iron rods in such a way as to show off the quality of the iron: half was hammered, and half was twisted; the hammered end was drawn to two points, and the twisted end sharpened into a blade. If iron could be worked in these four ways it was obviously of good quality. But the blacksmiths did not rely upon the quality of their metal or workmanship to ensure circulation—they gave each rod a "soul," which would be lost if it were broken. These iron rods were called *kilindi*.

The end with two points was called a *kodo*, "foot," and the blade end a *nileng*, "ear." In Sierra Leone the "ear" was later called a "wing," so that—with a wing and a foot—the money could travel!

From the beginning the Kissi were very particular about accepting kilindi and refused any having the least imperfection. Seeing both ends in place assured that the piece was of its original length and had not been "clipped." And, of course, if either end broke, the kilindi lost its soul, and had to be reincarnated by the medicine man of the tribe; a small fee was charged for this service.

But the blacksmiths themselves began making narrower and shorter pieces. The earliest kilindi were up to 30 inches long, and specimens collected in the 19th century are a minimum of 26 inches. By 1932 the average length was 18 inches, but pieces as short as 12 inches were known as early as 1944; still later ones shrank to 8 inches. Kilindi were replaced by coins in the mid-1950s.

Because kilindi were of comparatively low value they were generally tied in bundles of 20. About 1910 a cow could be purchased for 100 bundles, a virgin bride for 200 bundles, or a slave for 300. Native salt cost three kilindi per package, leading to another unit of account, *kpoloi* (a salt), equal to three pieces. A yard-long piece of native cloth (woven in a strip only four inches wide), 20 oranges, or several kola nuts cost two kilindi, and a child's loincloth only a single piece. Kilindi also acquired an exchange value in Western coins; from 1925 to 1929 a bundle of 20 pieces was equal to a shilling (so one kilindi was worth only 60 percent of a British penny, despite its nickname).[61]

Kissi pennies
(25% actual size)

Kissi penny bundle (30% actual size)

"Ogoja Penny"

Tribes in Southern Nigeria made Y-shaped iron currency bars, popularly known as "Ogoja pennies," but called by natives *yakaro* (Munshi tribe), *iyayaw* (Akuju tribe), or *efufy* (Nkumm tribe). In the first half of the 20th century, their value ranged from about a penny to less than a halfpenny.[62]

Ogoja penny (15% actual size)

Club (*Ensuba*)

Club (30% actual size)

In the Bizom tribe in Yokadouma, southeastern Cameroon, purchasing a bride in early pre-colonial times usually required 30 heavy club-shaped iron ingots (*ensuba*, a more or less general name for money among some tribes) weighing about 15 pounds each. Similarly-shaped iron money was used to the south, in Gabon and Angola.[63]

Iron Triangle (*Ensuba*)

Another form of "wife-buying money," also called *ensuba*, was a triangular-shaped piece of flat, brittle reworked iron over a foot long, with two notches near the point. These were used early in the 20th century by the Bafia tribe of the highlands of Cameroon, about 250 miles east of Yokadouma.[64]

Miniature Spearheads

The Yaunde tribe of Cameroon (a sub-tribe of the Pangwe) used miniature spearheads only 3 to 4 inches long, called *mimboss* or *mimbass*, as their currency.[65] They were of so little value that they circulated in bundles of about 75 pieces, and bride-price in the early 1930s was around 6,000

Iron triangle
(30% actual size)

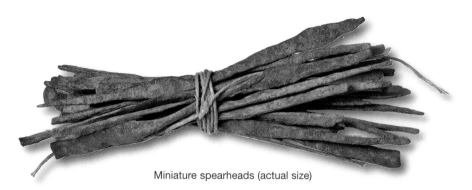

Miniature spearheads (actual size)

mimboss. It is supposed that mimboss originated centuries ago; they were used as money through the 1930s.

Yaunde men were passionately fond of a gambling game called *Abia*, which was played with chips carved from the poisonous nut of the poisonous fruit of the Elan tree. A finished chip cost about five mimboss, while the raw nut cost only two. Once a player lost 100 mimboss, according to the rules, he was *awu*—dead. A losing player who was unable to pay loans from the winners was sold into slavery at high noon the next day, unless ransomed by his family.

A less dangerous activity for a Yaunde man was visiting a friend, staying for about a month at a time, after which he was sent home with gifts such as mimboss, salt, and hats. This visit was reciprocated with equivalent gifts, facilitating exchanges (the Yaunde had no markets).[66]

Miniature Axeheads

Another branch of the Pangwe tribe, who lived in the Gabon "bush," preferred miniature axeheads called *bikĕi*. Somewhat larger than mimboss, they were usually put up in bundles of 10 or 12. They were common currency in the 1890s and were required for bride-price.[67]

Miniature axeheads (85% actual size)

STONE MONEY

Yap

Nothing is more curious than the stone money of Yap, a group of islands in the Caroline Islands archipelago. It gained its value because the stone had to be quarried on the island of Palau, 250 miles away, then shaped, drilled, and finished by hand, and finally transported to Yap by canoe or steamship.

Yapese oral tradition dates the introduction of stone money to about 1709, and this is supported by archaeology: an excavated stone disk about 4-3/8 inches in diameter, though without a hole, was carbon dated to 1756 (plus or minus 200 years, due to uncertainties in the Carbon 14 method, but it must be well before 1850). Massive stone money was first seen by Westerners in 1843, when a piece about two feet in diameter was presented by a chief of Palau to the chief of Yap.

The money stones are more or less round, with central holes for carrying. Their diameter varies from half-dollar size to about 12 feet. They are hewn from aragonite, usually whitish but sometimes with a yellowish or brownish color. The surface texture and shaping of the stone varies; some are extremely rough and porous, while others are polished to a very smooth, almost enamel-like finish.

Originally the money was quarried with primitive stone tools, drifted out to sea on large bamboo rafts, and transported back to Yap by canoes, a log laid across two canoes passing through the center of the stone. Once, when an enormous stone sank during a storm, all on the expedition testified on their return to its great value and that it was lost through no fault of its owners; consequently, they were recognized as being wealthy, even though their money was at the bottom of the sea.

With the arrival of European traders, iron tools were introduced and the stones began to be shipped on their vessels. Captain David Sean O'Keefe made a business of this trade, transporting Yapese to Palau from 1872 to 1901, where they hewed out their money. They then pawned it to O'Keefe for transport back to Yap, redeeming it on their return with copra. As a result, the size of the stones became larger and larger. Those brought by canoes and rafts were a maximum of 4 feet in diameter. O'Keefe started the quarrying of pieces up to 6 feet, which was as big as he could get into his holds. The very largest pieces were shipped after 1899 in German steamers.

Stone money was made as late as 1931. Total production was about 13,350, but about half of these have since been destroyed, chiefly during World War II.

When the Germans colonized Yap in the 1880s they found that there were no roads, and even the footpaths were in bad shape. They ordered the Yapese to improve them, but to no effect. Fines imposed were disregarded unless collected in stone money, so, taking advantage of the fact that the Yapese transferred title to their money without actually moving it, they marked some of the most valuable

Yap stones (20% actual size)

stones in black paint to show that the government had claimed them. The natives immediately improved the paths. Then, amid great rejoicing, the letters were erased, and the Yapese received their money back.

Since the stone money never had a set value, its status as money has been questioned. However, out of respect, Yapese expect to pay more when the seller

Collector Charles J. Opitz next to Yap stone

is a woman or an old man, and much exchange takes place by "giving" things away. Stone money was used as part of marriage exchange: the woman's side gave stone money, "a woman's valuable," and women's products such as food from the gardens, while the man's side gave shell money, "a man's valuable," and men's products such as fish, coconuts, and bananas. (Stone money is a woman's valuable because it stays at the estate, like a woman.) In modern Yap, stone money is often used as collateral for loans in U.S. currency to buy pickup trucks, boats, etc.[68]

Yap stone (12.5% actual size)

Togoland

Centrally-pierced stone money, though much smaller, was also used in Africa. Ancient, irregular quartzite spheres, about 2 to 3 inches in diameter—originally made between circa 500 BC and circa AD 500 and probably intended as fertility offerings *(heiliges geld)*—circulated as money in Togoland (now part of Ghana) in the latter part of the 19th century.[69] Large hoards have been found, leading to speculation that they were intended as money originally.[70]

Togoland stone (actual size)

OTHER TRADITIONAL MONEY

Rossel Island Money

In Rossel Island (Yela), 200 miles southeast of New Guinea, arose the most complex monetary system ever. First, it was gendered: there was men's money, *ndap*, and women's money, *nkö*, though—with a few minor differences—both kinds were used in the same way. Second, each kind had multiple "denominations": there were 22 different values of ndap

Rossel Island *ndap* (actual size)

Rossel Island *nkö* (80% actual size)

and 16 of nkö. However, the higher values of ndap were not simple multiples of the lower values, but perhaps equaled a lower value plus the equivalent of accumulated interest for a certain period. Third, ndap represented higher values than nkö, and its highest units were treated with reverence and rarely circulated; the 13 highest denominations of ndap had individual names. Fourth, the money supply of nkö was frozen, with no additional pieces being made; all existing specimens in use in the 1920s appeared to be very ancient. With such a restricted money supply, the economy of Rossel Island depended heavily on loans. The Rossel Islanders believed that their money was of supernatural origin.[71]

Ndap consists of somewhat triangular pieces of *Spondylus* shell, ground down and polished, and perforated near a rounded corner. Their value depends on the color, which varies from piece to piece. Nkö comprises sets of 10 irregular disks, probably from the shell of a giant clam. Several strings of tens can be assembled to make a higher value. Both continue to be used to buy pigs, houses, canoes, and garden crops.[72]

Sacred Shell Money (*Diwarra*)

Cords of *Nassa* shells with their backs broken, strung like beads on rattan strips up to 200 fathoms long, were the money of New Britain, and still pass as currency to buy local goods. This money was sacred and believed to have been created by spirits. On the Gazelle Peninsula, it was called tambu or tabu, but on Duke of York Island it was known as *diwarra*.[73]

Diwarra was the most highly-developed traditional currency of Oceania, used "in payment for goods and services of every description"; blood money required up to 50 strings, yet a few shells could be twisted off to purchase betel nuts. It was a measure of value, with most prices quoted regularly in diwarra. It was also a standard of deferred payment; there was an elaborate credit system in the Duke of York Island group, with

Diwarra (50% actual size)

interest normally at 10 percent. Finally, it was also an important store of value; in long coils, it was wealth, deposited in a sort of bank (stored with a moneylender).[74]

There was even a play-money version; children were taught how to use it, and made imitation diwarra of inferior shells to buy and sell among themselves.[75]

Beetle Leg Strings

On San Matthias Island, north of the Bismarck Archipelago, the brilliant peacock-blue joints of a beetle of the *Buprestidae* family were strung on stiff fiber or two-ply twine. Before World War I, one fathom of this colorful money equaled a German mark and could purchase a chicken.[76]

Beetle leg strings (2x actual size)

Red-Feather Money

For over a century, the only money used in the Santa Cruz Islands consisted of long, wide coils of glued-together bird feathers. Reportedly invented in the mid-1860s,[77] red-feather money was used to pay a fine for murder as early as 1871.[78] By 2000 it was no longer being made, though it was still used as a standard of value for bride-price.[79]

Each coil was made on order and required the efforts of three men: one to snare 300 scarlet honeyeater birds and

Red-feather money (10% actual size)

pluck their red feathers; another to shoot pigeons with bow and arrow, glue their feathers into a platelet, and trim them with the red feathers; and a third to bind each of 1,500 red-tipped platelets onto two cords of bark fiber such that they overlapped, so that the whole 30-foot coil seemed to be composed entirely of red feathers. A single coil took up to 600 man-hours of work.

Unfortunately, the red color disappears with time from wear and vermin damage, causing the coil to depreciate as it deteriorates. When completely colorless it is worthless and is discarded. But the value of a coil increases geometrically from the least valuable to the newest and best. Bride-price is always set at 10 coils, one of each quality, with the most valuable at the bottom of the pile and the least at the top, each coil being worth double that of the one above. Concubines could also be purchased with red feather money—but they cost 10 times as much.[80]

Woodpecker Scalps

Scalps of redheaded woodpeckers were used as money by several northern California Indian tribes, particularly the Yurok and Karok. They were essential for payments of blood money and bride-price. Their value depended upon size, with scalps from a larger and more brilliant species worth twice as much as those from a smaller. In 1872, the Karok valued these woodpecker scalps at $5 and $2.50, respectively.[81]

Woodpecker scalp (75% actual size)

Elephant Tails

In the Congo, it was the other end of the animal that was valuable, however: late in the 16th century, a single elephant tail could buy two or three slaves, and 50 hairs from the tail were worth 1,000 Portuguese reis. Elephant hairs were also a popular barter item in East Africa into the 20th century, though their use as actual currency has been questioned.[82]

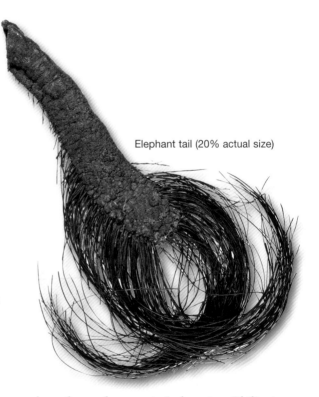

Elephant tail (20% actual size)

Human Skulls

Even human skulls have been used as a form of money in Indonesian, Philippine, and New Guinea head-hunting societies. They were highly valued, hoarded as treasures, used for bride-price, and accepted in payment of fines. In the ninth century, no man of Nias (off Sumatra) could marry unless he possessed the head of an enemy. If he had two heads, he could take two wives. In the 1420s, according to Venetian merchant Niccolò Da Conti, the cannibals of Battech, Sumatra,

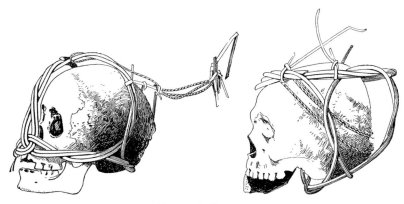

Human skull money

used heads "to purchase any article . . . and he who has the most heads in his house is considered to be most wealthy."[83]

Mats

Woven-fiber mats were currency throughout much of Melanesia and Micronesia well into the 20th century and are still used for bride-price.[84] In Samoa, fine mats—which take months or even years to make—circulated prior to the Second World War. Wages were paid in them, fines, blood-money and bride-price payments were fixed in them, and they were also the principal store of value.[85] In some islands in Vanuatu, mats made change for pigs, and—unlike red-feather money—*appreciated* as they got older; on Maewo they were kept in separate houses and continually smoked to darken them with soot. The darkest mats were so valuable they were only used to buy club advancement, and were never moved even when they changed ownership.[86]

Vanuatu mat (30% actual size)

Belts

When the mats of Oceania are sufficiently narrow, they are best described as belts or girdles. The girdles of Kosrae (Kusaie), in Eastern Micronesia, the most beautiful in all of Oceania, were too fine for actual use and were made early in the 20th century exclusively for presentation and exchange. Similar girdles were a form of currency in San Matthias, still finely woven, though less elaborate than those of Kosrae.[87]

San Mathias currency belt (30% actual size)

Shields

The island of Guadalcanal in the Solomon Islands used woven wicker shields as currency from the mid-19th century to 1980. Up to about 1880 these shields took the form of long ovals with almost parallel sides, but later began to be wider at one end, developing points at each end by circa 1910. One shield could purchase a wife.[88]

"Chief's coppers," roughly shaped like shields, were the equivalent of high-denomination bank notes among the Indians of the Northwest coast. Made of sheet copper, the larger sizes were decorated with figures. The biggest were nearly three feet high, and one of them—whose name meant "all other coppers are ashamed to look at it"—was worth 7,500 blankets in 1895. (At the time this equaled $3,750.) They were given away, or sometimes even destroyed, in potlatch ceremonies as a challenge to another tribe to prove who was wealthier.[89]

Guadalcanal shields (15% actual size)

Chief's copper (15% actual size)

COINS

The most common customary objects used as money, of course, are coins. Tired of weighing every nugget of native electrum panned from the Pactolus River, toward the end of the seventh century BC the Lydians began issuing electrum lumps already adjusted to their stater standard.

Lydian electrum lump (actual size)

At first, these coins were oval and simply had one to three square punches applied separately to one side and, on the other, striations from an anvil scored to hold the lump in place during striking. Soon a design and inscription were cut into the anvil. In the sixth century, King Croesus replaced the doubtful-quality electrum

Coins of Croesus (actual size)

with coins minted of pure gold or silver.[90] The ancient Greeks went on to replace the punches with a second design and to make the coins circular.

Bronze and other metals followed. After the Renaissance, machinery permitted the minting of larger and rounder coins with smooth, reeded, or lettered edges and noncircular shapes.[91]

Entirely independently, round bronze coins with a round central hole—but cast, not struck—were introduced in China during the Warring States Period, between circa 475 and circa 223 BC. Later the hole was made square for ease in taking the casting flash off the edge; a square rod through the center kept the coin from shifting during filing.[92]

Chinese square-holed cash coin (actual size)

Odd-Shaped Coins

Besides round, coins have been rectangular, oval, irregular ("cob"), square, scalloped, multi-sided, holed—even dolphin-shaped.[93]

Square coin, India (actual size)

Scalloped coin, Sudan (actual size)

Dolphin coin, Olbia (actual size)

Cup-Shaped Coins

Coins do not need to be flat, either: the Celts of Central Europe struck cup-shaped gold staters in the third and second centuries BC.[94] Circa AD 70 to circa AD 120, King 'Amdan Bayyin of the Himyarite dynasty of Yemen minted some very concave small silver coins.[95] It was left to the Byzantine Empire, however, to issue cup-shaped coins in all metals for over two hundred years, circa 1145 to 1352; this fabric was also copied in nearby Bulgaria and Hungary.[96] Concave, uni-face silver *hohlpfennigs* (hollow pfennigs) were also struck in parts of the Holy Roman Empire from about 1368 to 1600.[97]

Byzantine gold hyperpyron (actual size)

Himyarite coin (actual size)

Hohlphennig (actual size)

Bracteates

Soon after 1100, German rulers began minting their silver denars thinner and broader, to the point where they became mere foils called bracteates; in Thuringia in the late 12th century, a single gram of silver was expanded to make a uniface coin up to 2 inches across.[98] Because of the high relief, it was necessary to strike bracteates using wooden dies; several could be struck at a time. Bracteates are so light for their diameter that they can float on water.[99] Though they frequently bear attractive designs, they are very fragile. Bracteates were discontinued in the mid-14th century.[100]

Bracteate (actual size)

Oversize Coins

Monster coins several inches in diameter have been issued at times. Circa 300 BC Rome began casting bronze coins weighing up to one Roman pound of 12 ounces (almost 3/4 of a modern pound), over 2-3/4 inches in diameter. In little over a century, though, these *aes grave*, as they are called, were reduced in weight by 11/12.[101] Oversized silver and gold coins were made in 16th- and 17th-century Europe, for presentation purposes or for show: multiple thalers (up to 10) and multiple ducats (up to 105).[102] In 1586, Japanese shogun Toyotomi Hideyoshi introduced *obans*, oval gold plates 6-3/4 inches high with their value and the signature of the mint superintendent written on them in India ink.[103] The Mughal emperor Shah Jahan minted a 75-ounce gold coin in 1653.[104]

Aes grave (actual size)

Money Trees

The square-holed coins of the Far East, and the 19th-century brass coins of Morocco, were cast in "trees" of various sizes, then broken apart and the rough edges filed smooth. Some of these trees have been preserved intact, perhaps issued in that form for presentation.[105]

Money tree detail
(60% actual size)

Money tree
(35% actual size)

Cut Pieces of Coins

Cut halfpence and
farthing (actual size)

Cut quarter of cross
pistareen (actual size)

Cut Crusader gold (actual size)

In England circa 780 to 1279, the silver penny was virtually the only coin minted. For change, it was cut into halves (halfpence) and fourths (farthings).[106] The Spanish cross pistareen was similarly quartered in 18th-century America, as was the Spanish-American 8 reales or dollar.[107] In the Crusader kingdom of Jerusalem, circa 1137 to 1187, some baser gold coins were issued only in the form of cut-up pieces; they were given Latin inscriptions and designs to distinguish them from cuttings of pure gold Islamic coins, also used to for payments.[108]

Plugged Coins

Some thin silver dirhams of the Spanish Umayyad Dynasty (AD 756–912) had their weights increased after striking by cutting slots in the coin and inserting a silver ribbon.[109] In the early 1700s, underweight Spanish-American "cob" silver dollars were brought up to standard in the British North American colonies by plugging them with silver.[110] Later in the 18th century, gold coins were similarly plugged in the West Indies and the United States, certified by the addition of a goldsmith's touch.[111]

Plugged Spanish Umayyad dirham (actual size)

West Indies gold plugged coin (actual size)

Countermarked Coins

From ancient times until 1946, coins have been countermarked, officially or privately, to revalue them or validate them for circulation.[112]

Countermarked coins of
Panticapaeum, 4th century BC,
and Saudi Arabia, 1946 (actual size)

Bimetallic and Nonmetallic Coins

The Christian kings of Aksum (Ethiopia) minted bronze coins with the center of the cross or the king's portrait inlaid with gold from circa AD 350 to circa AD 550, seemingly as an embellishment like gold leaf on manuscripts.[113] About 1667, copper coins were struck for Ireland with a splash of brass inserted into the blank—making a crown appear to be gold—to thwart counterfeiting.[114] Italy introduced a bimetallic (aluminum-bronze center within a stainless steel ring) 500 lire coin in 1982, and somewhat similar bimetallic compositions are now used for all 1- and 2-euro coins.[115]

Aksum bronze coin with gold inlay (actual size)

St. Patrick's "halfpenny" (actual size)

During the siege of Leyden by Spain in 1574, the defenders struck paper coins made from Book of Hours leaves.[116] After Germany's defeat in World War I, Saxony issued a set of coins in Meissen porcelain.[117]

Leyden paper coin (actual size)

Saxony porcelain coin (actual size)

Trade Coins

Many countries minted special silver or gold coins primarily for external use. Among the most popular of these is the silver Maria Theresia thaler, which has been struck for the Arabian and Red Sea trade since 1780 with no change of date. Beginning in 1764, thalers were minted in Günzburg, Bavaria, to facilitate trade with the East. Those with the portrait of Maria Theresia were the most popular, so restrikes from the old dies were ordered after her death in 1780. When these wore out new dies were made, and have continued to be made ever since. In 1935, Mussolini demanded the dies from Austria to mint coins for his invasion of Ethiopia; Britain and France struck millions more between 1936 and 1941. Maria Theresia thalers circulated in Muscat and Oman until 1970.[118]

Maria Theresia thaler (actual size)

Another staple of international trade in the 18th and 19th centuries was the "piece of eight" or "Spanish milled dollar." Beginning in 1732, Spain began minting silver 8 reales coins by machinery at its mints in North and South America. These plentiful coins were widely accepted in Colonial America; the colony of Maryland switched to the dollar for its paper money in 1767, and on September 2, 1776, Thomas Jefferson recommended to the Continental Congress that the new country adopt the dollar as its monetary unit—which was done.[119]

Spanish dollars were highly desired in China also; those accepted as genuine were given a "chopmark" by Chinese merchants as a guarantee. After Mexico gained its independence in 1821, Mexican 8 reales replaced them in the Far East trade. They were so popular that "trade dollars" of equivalent value were made by several other countries during the 19th century, including the United States.[120]

Spanish milled dollar, Mexico City mint, 1734 (actual size)

6
MONEY SUBSTITUTES

Since money is sometimes inconvenient or risky to carry around, various substitutes have been devised over the centuries to use in lieu of actual cash. In many cases, they have become money in their own right.

Paper Money

The most universal of these substitutes is the bank note, or paper money. About AD 1000, merchants in the Sichuan region of China began to issue private notes made of mulberry paper as a substitute for local iron coins of low value. After payment was refused on some issues, the government in 1023 took over their emission.[1] Wrote Marco Polo 275 years later, "paper currency is circulated in every part of the great khan's dominions; nor dares any person, at the peril of his life, refuse to accept it in payment. . . . With it . . . every article may be procured."[2]

Ming Dynasty note
(15% actual size)

In the West, it was gold, not iron, that was represented by paper. Merchants began to deposit their gold with goldsmiths for safekeeping. The receipts for these deposits were a more convenient way to settle accounts than drawing out the gold again, and they achieved limited circulation. Soon the goldsmiths recognized that not all receipts

would be presented at once, and that it would be safe to issue notes for more than the amount of gold on hand. By making loans in the form of these notes, against reserves of less than 100 percent, some English goldsmiths transformed themselves into banks early in the Commonwealth period, circa 1650.[3]

The first true bank notes, however, were those of the Stockholms Banco, issued in 1661, declared by royal decree to be freely

Stockholms Banco note
(25% actual size)

5 Euro, Israeli 10 Lirot,
Croatian 5 Dinara notes
(50% actual size)

Hong Kong 1-cent note (75% actual size)

circulating legal tender.[4] These Swedish bank notes unleashed a flood of imitators, to the point where government-issued paper money is the universal currency of the civilized world.

Paper money has been issued in denominations from 1 Hong Kong cent to 100 quintillion (100,000,000,000,000,000,000) Hungarian pengös.[5] Since paper money is inexpensive to produce, its adoption without restraint has led to a series of horrific inflations: among others, colonial America, 1713 to 1781;[6] France, 1719 and 1720[7] and again, 1790 to 1796;[8] Confederate States of America, 1861 to 1865; Germany, 1920 to 1923; Hungary, 1945 to 1946;[9] and now Zimbabwe.

Confederate $100 note (35% actual size)

Zimbabwe $100 trillion note (45% actual size)

Many steps have been taken to protect against counterfeiting, among them threats ("To Counterfeit is DEATH"), counterfoils (stubs bearing the same serial number, to be irregularly cut), fine paper, fine engraving, colored inks, watermarks, colored fibers or disks embedded in the paper, diffuse colored shadings, embedded metal or plastic strips, microprinting, color-shifting ink, and holograms. None have been totally effective, even for a short time.[10]

Continental currency note
(80% actual size)

"Paper" Money

A number of materials have been substituted for paper in notes over the years, either to make them longer lasting, out of necessity, or (in some cases) for sheer novelty.

Short of coins with which to pay troops defending against the Iroquois, Jacques de Meulles, intendant of New France, took drastic action in 1685. He requisitioned all the packs of playing cards possessed by the army and the merchants, cut them in quarters, wrote denominations on them, signed them (the governor also signed the higher values), applied seals, and paid the troops with

Austrian playing card money (75% actual size)

them. Though intended as a temporary expedient until the arrival of funds in a few months, card money proved so acceptable that many further issues were made; it was made legal tender by the king of France in 1729 and issued as late as 1757.[11] It was also used in Louisiana from 1722 to about 1790[12] and in Austria and Germany after the First World War.[13]

The Russian American Company issued a local currency for Alaska in 1816, originally on cardboard, but switched to parchment in 1826 for greater durability. A few later notes may even have been printed on Alaskan walrus hide. Despite this, the parchment notes rarely lasted more than a couple of years in the rugged Alaskan environment before the printing and serial numbers disappeared.[14]

Cloth has also been resorted to. In 1902, during the Boer War, British field commanders hand wrote and rubber-stamped promissory notes on any fabric available.[15] The Sichuan-Shaanxi Worker-Peasant Bank printed some of its notes on cotton cloth from 1933 to 1935, because of the poor quality of paper available in that remote area of China.[16] German cities and towns issued cloth *notgeld* (emergency money) notes during World War I and the following inflation period, 1915 to 1923. The earliest issues seem to

Alaskan parchment note (actual size)

Chinese cloth note (75% actual size)

be true necessity money, but after 1920 they were mere fund-raising souvenirs. After linen came silk; after silk, burlap and even velvet.[17]

The search for durable currency has led dozens of countries to replace paper with plastic. The earliest, Haiti, issued a 50 gourde note in 1980 printed on DuPont Tyvek®; Costa Rica and the Isle of Man soon followed. Though the material itself had 20 times the life expectancy of paper, the issue was not successful because of poor ink retention, and all three countries reverted to paper. Polymer, and hybrid paper/polymer, proved superior; polymer lasts four times longer than paper, and most countries have continued to use it. Polymer notes are nonporous, so they stay cleaner than paper notes, an advantage in the tropics. Some polymer notes took advantage of its unique properties, such as a Brunei 1 dollar issued in February 1996 incorporating a transparent area within the design; other notes include holograms.[18]

Polymer notes (85% actual size)

Private Coins

During the Georgia, North Carolina, California, and Colorado gold rushes of the 19th century, far from the U.S. Mint or branch mints of the time, private persons minted gold coins as an alternative to the circulation of gold dust. Denominations ranged from 25¢ to huge $50 "slugs." Private mints were abolished by the Coinage Act of April 22, 1864.[19]

Victor, Colorado, silver booster Joseph Lesher issued silver "Referendum Souvenirs" in 1900 and 1901, in octagonal form so as to avoid imitating U.S. silver dollars. The 1900 issues even bore the odd denomination of $1.25, though this was changed to $1.00 the following year. However, the Secret Service seized his first dies, and each later issue plainly stated that it was redeemable at only one business.[20]

Nearly a century later, another libertarian hard-money advocate, Bernard von NotHaus, founded NORFED (National Organization for the Repeal of the Federal Reserve Act and Internal Revenue Code). In 1998, following a favorable opinion from the Treasury's Bureau of Engraving and Printing, he began issuing .999 silver one troy ounce "Liberty Dollars" (actual face value $10, a significant premium over their silver value at the time) and paper warehouse receipts. Face values were doubled in 2005 as the price of silver rose, but then reports were received of Liberty Dollars being passed on unsuspecting salesclerks as U.S. coins. Despite von NotHaus modifying the design, a different division of the Treasury (the U.S. Mint) declared silver Liberty Dollars illegal; the FBI raided the firm November 15, 2007, and seized its entire stock.[21]

1851 $50 gold slug
(actual size)

Lesher dollar (actual size)

$10 Liberty Dollar (actual size)

Leather Money

Leather has been used as money from ancient Rome to 1934, often as a result of wars and their aftermath. During the Crusades, in 1122 and 1124, Venetian Doge Domenico Michaele paid his fleet and troops with squares of leather cut from horsehides and stamped with his seal; they

Austrian leather money (actual size)

were called *Michaeletta* after him. The Dutch defenders of Leyden in 1574 resorted to cutting up the leather bindings of old books and stamping a device on them. This money did not remain in circulation, however, as the starving citizens boiled and ate them![22]

After World War I, Mattighofen, Austria, authorized a leather factory to stamp half-moon-shaped 1 krone pieces and round 10 heller pieces from scrap sole leather.[23] In the inflation that followed, however, the residents—after first using leather for money—turned the tables and used money for leather, making soles for paper shoes from these pieces, as it was cheaper than to buy new leather soles.[24]

Bamboo Money

Private bamboo tokens were first produced in China in 1238. However, use was most widespread from about 1877 to 1936; traveling merchants then made them more liquid by discounting them by 5 percent. During the Japanese occupation, bamboo tokens returned, issued by small firms and municipalities.[25] Among them, the (Japanese puppet) Wuxi City Office issued 1 and 5 copper dollar bamboo tokens in 1939.[26]

Chinese bamboo money (70% actual size)

Counterfeit Coins and Paper Money

Almost from the beginning of coinage, dishonest people have counterfeited or diminished ("clipped") money. Forgeries merely plated with silver are known of ancient Greek coins, and governments today strive to stay ahead of counterfeiters.

In times of great coin shortages, though, known counterfeits have been tolerated in circulation. In fact, counterfeit coins were actually made a legal tender in Martinique: false sou marqués (imitations of base silver French Colonial double sols stamped with a crowned C, but absent the silver) were prohibited from circulation in 1797, but six months later, "on account of the small number of good pieces on the island," they were allowed by decree "provisionally" to pass at 10 deniers each.[27]

Counterfeit
sou marqué
(actual size)

Because of the greater opportunity for profit, paper money has been heavily counterfeited from the start. In the United States between the end of the Revolution and the end of Civil War, it consisted of more than 10,000 varieties of bank notes, currency issued by private banks. From 10 to 50 percent of the money in circulation was worthless, either issued by failed (broken) banks or outright forgeries. Merchants coped by consulting "counterfeit detectors," books describing the characteristics of genuine and counterfeit notes—or by keeping the fakes moving. An editorial in the *Bloomington (IL) Weekly Pantagraph*, June 10, 1857, admitted, "it is a favorite maxim with some to 'keep bad money in circulation,' for they say it makes no difference whether a bill is counterfeit or not, so long as it will pass around freely."[28]

Counterfeit Massachusetts
bank note (70% actual size)

Bills of Exchange

Bills of exchange, documents prepared (or sold) at one place and payable at another, often with a delay in payment similar to a promissory note, were invented by the merchants of Babylon early in the second millennium

Printed bill of exchange (40% actual size)

BC. In the medieval Mediterranean world, Jewish merchants depended upon bills of exchange, *suftaja* in Persian, for long distance commerce. Muslim lawyers defined a suftaja as a "loan of money in order to avoid the risk of transport," a good definition today; the Jewish merchants of the 11th century and later drew them on well-known bankers, paying a fee for their issue, and they were subject to a daily penalty if not paid promptly, like modern bills of exchange.[29]

The Genoese independently wrote bills of exchange as early as 1156, and printed forms appeared in the 18th century. In gold-rush California, bills of exchange were the preferred way of transferring funds to the East Coast and abroad.[30] Modern traveler's checks—devised by the American Express Company in 1891—are their successors.[31]

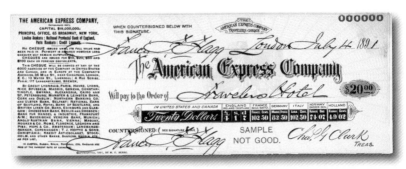

American Express Travelers Cheque (50% actual size)

Checks

Closely related to bills of exchange, and apparently of about equal antiquity, are checks, written orders instructing a holder of the check writer's funds to pay them to another. Their form and shape have changed little since the 1780s. However, their usage is declining rapidly with the advent of credit and debit cards.[32]

Early check (55% actual size)

Abernethy's Rock Money

Oregon City (Oregon Territory) pioneer merchant George Abernethy made change in his general store in 1844 by gluing miniature promissory notes to chips of flint discarded by Indians.[33]

Abernethy's 35 cents rock money

Tokens

Privately-issued coin-like objects—tokens—have been used as substitutes for coins since antiquity, especially as gaming chips and petty currency. In the Middle Ages, pewter and lead tokens were cast by church authorities and private merchants in Europe to aid pilgrims and to make change for the smallest coins.[34] During the Depression, for sales tax payments of less than a cent, 12 U.S. states issued tokens of one to five mills (thousandths of a dollar). Tokens have been made of every material from gold to cardboard.[35]

Tokens (actual size)

Siamese Porcelain Gambling Tokens

Though gambling was a favorite pastime in 18th-century Siam (modern Thailand), the round bullet money had an annoying tendency to roll away when thrown to the croupier. The Siamese solution was for the gambling houses *(hongs)* to make colorful porcelain tokens of various shapes for the use of their patrons. As the hongs were licensed by the government, their convenient tokens achieved general circulation. They were finally prohibited in 1917.[36]

Siamese porcelain gambling tokens (actual size)

Wooden Nickels

While rectangular wooden *notgeld* notes were issued in Austria in 1920, the true "wooden nickel" came about following the failure of the Citizens Bank of Tenino, Washington, in 1931. The Tenino Chamber of Commerce issued scrip (notes entitling the holder to receive something) against the frozen deposits, printed on slices of local spruce wood. Further issues followed and were imitated across America, primarily as festival souvenirs. Since 1954 most wooden nickels have been round.[37]

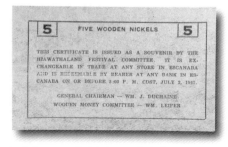

Wooden nickels (square nickels 55% actual size; round nickel actual size)

California Clamshell Money

Following the bank holiday proclaimed by the governor of California on March 1, 1933, two small California communities began using clamshells for money. The Crescent City Chamber of Commerce immediately issued scrip handwritten on clamshells, in denominations of 10¢ and 25¢; later four local businesses did also. When the banks reopened March 13, all clamshells presented were paid in full.

On Monday morning, March 6, William H. Bogue, who had a cigar store across the street from K.L. Phillips's service station in Pismo Beach, tried to buy a roll of nickels from Phillips for change. Phillips had none to spare and laughingly said, "Oh, well, don't worry, we can always use clamshells for money until the banks open." Bogue then made a piece of clamshell scrip as a joke, and Phillips accepted it and put it in his store window. After a customer bought it, unemployed citizens were soon making more clamshell money. There were a dozen Pismo Beach issuers in all, with values from 25¢ to $20.[38]

Pismo Beach, California, clamshell money (60% actual size)

Labor Money

British reformer Robert Owen urged making "equal values of labor" the "only equitable principle" of trade, and founded an equitable labor exchange in London in 1832 at which goods could be exchanged for notes payable in hours of labor. A second exchange opened in 1833 in Birmingham, and communities were established in America in the 1830s on the same principle, but the system survived only a short time.[39]

Exactly a century later, a similar currency was introduced by the Unemployed Relief Club, Inc., of Waterloo, Iowa. For a membership fee of 10¢, men could work in fields or logging camps in exchange for scrip valued in hours of labor, which could be spent for food and fuel.[40]

National Equitable Labour Exchange note (40% actual size)

Unemployed Relief Club note (50% actual size)

Local Currencies (LETS and CCC)

After the 1980s recession led to high unemployment in Courtenay, British Columbia, activist Michael Linton founded a Local Employment and Trade System in 1983. LETS used a "green dollar" currency to put barter on a nonprofit,

HOURS note
(45% actual size)

community-wide basis. Worldwide, about 200 other complementary community currencies (CCC) have been issued, and "LETS" now stands for Local Exchange Trading Systems.[41]

Among these are Ithaca (NY) HOURS, founded during the 1991 recession to promote "local economic strength . . . and social justice, ecology, community participation, and human aspirations." One HOUR equals $10 and can be used to buy alternative healing, mind/body therapy, yoga instruction, singing telegrams—even activism.[42]

Wire Transfers

In 1871, Western Union introduced a service to send money by telegram, though at first it was used only in emergencies because of its expense. The 12 Federal Reserve Banks began transferring balances among each other and the Treasury using Morse code in 1918, and after many changes this has become the modern Fedwire system.[43] An international system, SWIFT (Society for Worldwide Interbank Financial Telecommunication), founded in Brussels in 1973 by banks from 15 countries, went live in 1977.[44] Together, these systems permit money seemingly to disappear from one place and to reappear (perhaps in a different currency) in another, miles or even continents away.[45] Even wireless payment is available, using a cellular telephone.

After several false starts, the modern Automatic Teller Machine (ATM) was introduced in 1971; three years later, ATMs went on-line, allowing money to be withdrawn far from the bank where it had been deposited.[46] Like wire transfers, foreign exchange is also possible.

Credit and Debit Cards

Merchants in Europe and the United States began issuing metal "charge coins" to customers about 1900, but it was not until 1958, when American Express and BankAmericard (now Visa) introduced plastic credit cards, that purchases could be made at a wide range of businesses without using money. Magnetic strips were added to cards (including ATM cards) in 1969; holograms and other security devices soon followed. Today there are many networks of credit card issuers.[47]

The debit card, a credit card lookalike that offers no credit but draws money from the user's account immediately, was introduced in Britain in 1988 and has since spread worldwide, with considerable variation. In many countries more debit than credit cards are in use.

These cards do not even need to be physically present for trade to occur; the card number can be sent over the Internet at any hour of the day or night to an online retailer who has no "brick and mortar" store, and the purchase will be consummated and the goods shipped.[48]

Credit cards (45% actual sizes)

Smart Cards and Stored-value Cards

In 1982 France introduced the Télécarte—a card with an embedded integrated circuit—for use in pay phones. Nine years later, all French debit cards had this feature. Not long afterwards, stored-value cards, which contain a preauthorized amount of money, were introduced (though they do not require the computer chip). The next innovation was the contactless smart card, using a wireless technology that permits the card simply to be touched to a reader or passed by a scanner. It may not even be necessary to take the card out of your wallet![49]

e-gold® and PayPal™

Many systems have been set up to facilitate payments over the World Wide Web. Perhaps the first was e-gold, introduced in 1996. It is accounted by weight and is said to be 100-percent backed by gold bullion in allocated storage.[50] Two years later, PayPal was founded; now operating in nearly 200 markets and 17 currencies, it allows users to send and receive money inexpensively without sharing financial information.[51]

Bank-created (Book Entry) Money

Subject to the constraints of its reserves, any bank can (and does) "create" money, simply by crediting the proceeds of a loan to the debtor's account. This newly-created money can be spent by check just like the government-issued money held in the bank's reserves.[52] Credit cards work similarly, allowing users to monetize future income.[53]

Invisible Money

Money declared to be so by government degree (fiat)—without intrinsic value of any kind—is defined as fiat money. In 1971, President Nixon repudiated the obligation of the United States to redeem dollars for gold, adding the U.S. to the list of fiat-money countries; by March 1973, all leading currencies had floating exchange rates.[54] Modern money is thus far less substantial than the money of our ancestors. Like the Holy of Holies—when you draw back the curtain, there is nothing there, just the "full faith and credit" of the issuing country. But, as Alan Greenspan said, it all comes down to trust—if you trust it, it's money!

NOTES

Chapter 1

1. Joe Cribb, *Money—From Cowrie Shells to Credit Cards* (London: British Museum Publications, 1986), 12.
2. Alan Greenspan, "The History of Money." (opening remarks, American Numismatic Society Exhibition, Federal Reserve Bank of New York, Jan. 16, 2002), http://www.federalreserve.gov /Boarddocs/speeches/2002/200201163/default.htm (accessed July 27, 2007).
3. Summarized in Michael Hudson, "The Creditary/Monetarist Debate in Historical Perspective," presented at the New School, New York, 1999, http://www.michael-hudson.com/articles /monetary/03CreditaryMonetaristDebate.html (accessed Aug. 19, 2008).
4. *Life*, Apr. 25, 1949, 100, quoted in Walter W. Haines, *Money, Prices, and Policy*, 2nd ed. (New York: McGraw-Hill Book Company, 1966), 18.
5. William Davenport, "Red-Feather Money," *Scientific American*, Mar. 1962, 95.

Chapter 2

1. Aristotle *Nicomachean Ethics* (1133a29–33, bk. V, ch. 5).
2. Craig Byron, "Perspectives: A Description of Fossil Hominids and Their Origins," Archaeology.Info, http://www.archaeologyinfo.com/perspectives004.htm (accessed Sept. 19, 2008).
3. Michael W. Pitts, *Later Stone Implements* (Aylesbury: Shire Archaeology, 1980), 11–15.
4. Ibid., 11, 32–34; Kenneth P. Oakley, *Man the Tool-Maker*, 6th ed. (Chicago: University of Chicago Press, 1976), 19; British Museum, Department of Prehistoric and Romano-British Antiquities. *Man before Metals* (London: British Museum Publications Ltd., 1979), 20–21; Paul Craddock and Mike Cowell, "Cutting Edge." *British Archaeology*, Nov. 2004, http://www.britarch.ac.uk/ba /ba79/feat2.shtml (accessed Sept. 19, 2008).
5. Tristan T. Almazan, Stephen E. Nash, and Lauren Zych, "The Field Museum Hopewell Catalogue Project: Getting the Word Out." *Hopewell Archeology* 6:1 (Sept. 2004), http://www.nps.gov /history/mwac/hopewell/v6n1/three.htm (accessed July 20, 2007); Stephen E. Nash and Jonathan R. Haas, "Mounds, Myths and Museums: The Hopewell Culture of Central Ohio, 100 BC–AD 400," *In The Field*, Nov.–Dec. 2000.
6. O.H. Dodson, "A Prehistoric Currency of the Hopewell Indians," *The Numismatist*, June 1951.
7. Three preserved in author's collection. Information supplied by John Smith.
8. Gary A. Wright, *Obsidian Analysis and Prehistoric Near Eastern Trade: 7500 to 3500 BC* (Ann Arbor: University of Michigan, 1969).
9. James Mellaart, "A Neolithic City in Turkey," repr. from *Scientific American*, 1964.
10. Smithsonian Institution, Smithsonian Museum of Natural History, Hall of Western Civilization, "The First Wholesalers?" exhibit, July 1986.
11. Dana Facaros and Michael Pauls, *Sicily* (London: Cadogan Guides, 1998), 148–149; Fionn Davenport, *Sicily* (Hawthorn, Victoria: Lonely Planet Publications, Ltd., 2000), 151.
12. John E. Clark and Thomas A. Lee Jr., "Formative Obsidian Exchange and the Emergence of Public Economies in Chiapas, Mexico," in *Trade and Exchange in Early Mesoamerica*, ed. Kenneth G. Hirth (Albuquerque: University of New Mexico Press, 1984), 235–274; Marcus C. Winter, "Exchange in Formative Highland Oaxaca," in *Trade and Exchange*, 179–185; Kenneth G. Hirth, "Trade and Society in Late Formative Morelos," in *Trade and Exchange*, 125–146; Robert S. Santley, "Obsidian Exchange, Economic Stratification, and the Evolution of Complex Society in the Basin of Mexico," in *Trade and Exchange*, 43–80; Michael W. Spence, "Craft Production and Polity in Early Teotihuacan," in *Trade and Exchange*, 87–114.
13. Charles J. Opitz, *An Ethnographic Study of Traditional Money* (Ocala: First Impressions Printing, Inc., 2000), 243.
14. Daniel C. Snell, *Ledgers and Prices, Early Mesopotamian Merchant Accounts* (New Haven and London: Yale University Press, 1982).
15. L.W. King, trans., "Hammurabi's Code of Laws," laws 215–217, http://eawc.evansville.edu /anthology/hammurabi.htm (accessed Sept. 16, 2008).
16. Miriam S. Balmuth, "The Monetary Forerunners of Coinage in Phoenicia and Palestine," in *International Numismatic Convention, Jerusalem, 27–31 December 1963: The Patterns of Monetary Development in Phoenicia and Palestine in Antiquity. Proceedings*, ed. A. Kindler (Tel Aviv: Schocken

Publishing House, 1967), 25–32, pl. I–VI.; Miriam S. Balmuth, ed. *Hacksilver to Coinage: New Insights into the Monetary History of the Near East and Greece, Numismatic Studies No. 24* (New York: The American Numismatic Society, 2001); John H. Kroll, "Observations on Monetary Instruments in Pre-Coinage Greece," in *Hacksilver to Coinage*, ed. Miriam S. Balmuth, 77; Bryan O. Burke Jr., "The Invention of Coins," *Selections from* The Numismatist, *Ancient and Medieval Coins*, repr. from Sept. 1959 issue (Racine, WI: Whitman Publishing Company, 1960), 9–22.

17. Robert D. Leonard Jr., "A Numismatic Illustration of the Bible," *Coin World's World Coins* Dec. 1987, S-6, S-10, S-12.
18. Länsmuseet På Gotland (The Historical Museum, Gotland), "Introduction, Hoards from the Early Viking Period, Hoards from the Late Viking Period," http://www.gotmus.i.se/1engelska/skatter/engelska/introduction.htm (accessed June 28, 2007).
19. Gareth Williams and Leslie Webster, "The Cuerdale Hoard," http://www.bbc.co.uk/history/ancient/vikings/cuerdale_01.shtml (accessed Sept. 14, 2008).
20. A.M. Rackus, "Origin of the Ruble," in *Selections from* The Numismatist: *Modern Foreign Coins*, repr. from April 1934 issue (Racine, WI: Whitman Publishing Co., 1961), 192–194.
21. Qian Jiaju, *A History of Chinese Currency: 16th Century BC–20th Century AD* (Hong Kong: Xinhua [New China] Publishing House, N.C.N. Limited, and M.A.O. Management Group Ltd., 1983), 35–36.
22. Opitz, *Traditional Money*, 322–323; A. Hingston Quiggin, *A Survey of Primitive Money—The Beginnings of Currency* (London: Methuen & Co., Ltd., 1978), 246–248.
23. Reginald Le May, *The Coinage of Siam* (Bangkok: The Siam Society, 1932, repr. 1977), 8–9; Quiggin, *Primitive Money*, 256–258; Opitz, *Traditional Money*, 246.
24. Andrew Sherratt, comp., "Ancient Times: An archaeological map and timescale for Europe Western Asia and Egypt." Oxford: Ashmolean Museum Dept. of Antiquities, 1985.
25. Morris Silver, review of *The Heqanakht Papyri*, by James P. Allen, Economic History Services, http://eh.net/bookreviews/library/0868 (accessed October 19, 2008); I.E.S. Edwards, C.J. Gadd, N.G.L. Hammond, and E. Sollberger, *The Cambridge Ancient History*, 3rd ed., vol. 2, part 1, *History of the Middle East and the Aegean Region c. 1800--1380 BC* (Cambridge: Cambridge University Press, 1973), 58, 351, 381–385, 389–390, 486–491.
26. Col. James W. Curtis, "Media of Exchange in Ancient Egypt" in *Selections from* The Numismatist, *Ancient and Medieval Coins*, repr. from May 1951 issue (Racine, WI: Whitman Publishing Company, 1960), 156–159.
27. "Cyprus: Brief History," Kypros.com, http://www.kypros.com/Cyprus/cyhistory.htm (accessed Sept. 19, 2008); Edwards, *Ancient History*, 574, 578, 649.
28. The Ashmolean Museum of Art and Archaeology, "Ancient Cyprus in the Ashmolean Museum: The Copper Trade: Ingots, Hoards and Ship Wrecks," The Ashmolean Museum, http://www.ashmolean.org/ash/amulets/cypruscopper/AncCyp-Cu-05.html (accessed Sept.18, 2008); George F. Bass, "Oldest Known Shipwreck Reveals Splendors of the Bronze Age," *National Geographic*, Dec. 1987; George F. Bass, *Archaeology Under Water* (New York: Frederick A. Praeger, 1966), 36–37, 139–142.
29. Michael H. Crawford, *Coinage and Money Under the Roman Republic* (Berkeley: University of California Press, 1985), 1–24; Jonathan Williams, ed., with Joe Cribb and Elizabeth Errington, *Money: A History* (New York: St. Martin's Press, 1997), 39–40; Vecchi, V.C. & Sons, "Certificate of Authenticity," London, Dec. 12, 1980.
30. William Geddes, *Per Aes et Libram.* (Liverpool: The University Press, 1952).
31. Williams, *Money: A History*, 40.
32. O.P. Eklund, *Copper Coins of Sweden*: Miss Berta Holmberg, *Coinage of Swedish Plate Money*, repr. from *The Numismatist* (Salina, Kansas: Olympic Press, n.d).
33. Opitz, *Traditional Money*, 251–252.
34. Edwards, *Ancient History*, 351; Mark Andrews, "The Private Tomb of Rekhmire on the West Bank at Luxor (ancient Thebes)," http://www.touregypt.net/featurestories/rekhmire.htm (accessed May 19, 2008); Brigitte Goede and Jon Hirst, "TT343, the Tomb of Benia," http://www.osirisnet.net/tombes/nobles/benia/e_benia_02.htm (accessed May 18, 2008).
35. R.A. Stewart Macalister, *Excavations at Gezer II, III* (London: Palestinian Exploration Fund, 1912) 259, Fig. 405.
36. Homer *Iliad* (bk. 23, lines 90–93, 262–270, 750–754).
37. Kroll, "Monetary Instruments," 77–79.
38. *Encyclopædia Britannica*, 14th ed., revised, s.v. "Gold."

39. Rev. W.L. Bevan, *The Student's Manual of Ancient Geography*, ed. William Smith (London: John Murray, 1864), 105; William Smith, *A Classical Dictionary of Biography, Mythology, and Geography* (London: John Murray, 1873), 197, 510; Dana Facaros and Michael Pauls, *Turkey* (London: Cadogan Guides, 2000), 239.
40. J.C.F. Johnson, *Getting Gold*, 2nd ed., revised (London: Charles Griffin & Company, 1898).
41. Peter G. Van Alfen, "Filthy Lucre," *Odyssey*, Sept.–Oct. 2004, 6–7.
42. Margaret Shinnie, *Ancient African Kingdoms* (1965; repr., New York: Mentor, 1970), 56–69.
43. Ibid., 109.
44. Paul Einzig, *Primitive Money in its Ethnological, Historical and Economic Aspects* (London: Eyre & Spottiswoode, 1948, repr. 1951), 153–154; Margaret Webster Plass, *African Miniatures—Goldweights of the Ashanti.* (New York: Frederick A. Praeger, 1967), 10.
45. David Williams, *The Georgia Gold Rush—Twenty-Niners, Cherokees, and Gold Fever* (Columbia, SC: University of South Carolina Press, 1993), 97.
46. Frank Soulé, John H. Gihon, M.D., and James Nisbet, *The Annals of San Francisco* (New York: D. Appleton & Co., 1855), 214–215.
47. *San Francisco Alta California*, "Bogus Dust," Oct. 26, 1851, 2.
48. Don Taxay, *Counterfeit, Mis-Struck, and Unofficial U.S. Coins* (New York: Arco, 1963), 170.
49. Einzig, *Primitive Money*, 95, 99–100, 104–105, 173, 295.
50. Associated Press, "Gold rush in Amazon rain forest," *Chicago Tribune*, Nov. 30, 1988.
51. *Encyclopædia Britannica*, 14th ed. revised, s.v. "Archaeology."
52. Plutarch *Lycurgus*, 9; Plutarch *Lysander*, 20; Einzig, *Primitive Money*, 231–233.
53. *Herodotus*, trans. Henry Cary (New York: Harper & Brothers, 1870) 2.135 (149); Kroll, "Monetary Instruments," 77–79; William Ridgeway, *The Origin of Metallic Currency and Weight Standards* (Cambridge: The University Press, 1892), 214.
54. Julius Caesar, *Commentarii de Bello Gallico* (Book V, Chapter 12:4, author's translation).
55. Quiggin, *Primitive Money*, 288–289; Marjorie & C.H.B. Quennell, *Everyday Life in the New Stone, Bronze & Early Iron Ages*, 2nd. ed. (London: B.T. Batsford, Ltd., 1931), Fig. 3, 112–113.
56. Einzig, *Primitive Money*, 99, 102–103, 114.

Chapter 3
1. Homer *Iliad* (bk. 6, lines 235–240).
2. Ibid. (bk. 23, lines 700–710).
3. Einzig, *Primitive Money*, 234.
4. Ibid., 117.
5. Ibid., 120–171, specifically 126–127; Isaac Schapera, *A Handbook of Tswana Law and Custom: Compiled for the Bechuanaland Protectorate Administration* (LIT Verlag Berlin-Hamburg-Münster, 1994), 138–140.
6. Sahih Bukhari, *The Sunnah*, trans. M. Muhsin Khan, vol. 5, bk. 58:185, vol. 9, bk. 83:36.http://www.usc.edu/dept/MSA/fundamentals/hadithsunnah/bukhari/ (accessed Sept. 19, 2008).
7. Einzig, *Primitive Money*, 102, 115–116; Quiggin, *Primitive Money*, 212; Opitz, *Traditional Money*, 248–250.
8. James Hookway, "Bad Diagnosis—In Rural Cambodia, Avian Influenza Finds a Weak Spot," *The Wall Street Journal* Mar. 4, 2005, A1, A10.
9. Einzig, *Primitive Money*, 56, 186; Don Taxay, *Money of the American Indians and other primitive currencies of the Americas* (Flushing: Nummus Press, 1970), 54; Nauru is in Micronesia, 26 miles south of the equator.
10. Einzig, *Primitive Money*, 210–215, 445, 448.
11. Ibid., 218–219.
12. Ibid., 256.
13. Ibid., 248.
14. Ibid., 103, 313–315.
15. Ibid., 145, 282.
16. Ibid., 183, 185–186, 292–293; Sylvester S. Crosby, *The Early Coins of America* (Boston, 1875: repr., 1975), 26; Sarah Knight, "Madame Knight's Journal," in *Narratives of Colonial America, 1704–1765*, ed. Howard H. Peckham (Chicago: The Lakeside Press, 1971), 5–49.
17. *Encyclopædia Britannica*, 14th ed., revised, s.v. "Slavery"; Homer *Iliad* (bk. 9, lines 260–275); B. Precourt, "The Trojan War," *Classical Mythology. Classics 171, Audio-Visual Supplement* (University of

Wisconsin–Milwaukee), http://www.uwm.edu/Course/mythology/1100/twar1.htm (accessed Sept. 19, 2008).

18. Einzig, *Primitive Money*, 247–248.
19. Quiggin, *Primitive Money*, 212.
20. Verney Lovett Cameron, *Across Africa* (New York: Harper and Brothers, 1877), 264–267.
21. Opitz, *Traditional Money*, 20.
22. Einzig, *Primitive Money*, 82.
23. Opitz, *Traditional Money*, 19.
24. Einzig, *Primitive Money*, 198.
25. Quiggin, *Primitive Money*, 276; Sabine Gerloff, Svend Hansen, and Felix Oehler, eds., *Die Funde der Bronzezeit aus Frankreich* (Berlin: Museum für Vor- und Frühgeschichte, 1993), 69–70; Neritan Ceka, *The Illyrians to the Albanians* (Tirana: Publishing House Migjeni, 2005), 47.
26. A.W. Putnam, *History of Middle Tennessee, or Life and Times of Gen. James Robertson* (1859; repr., Knoxville: University of Tennessee Press, 1971), 320n.
27. Museo del Banco Central del Ecuador, Manta, "Hachas monedas" exhibit, Nov. 18, 2007; Dorothy Hosler, Heather Lechtman, and Olof Holm, *Axe-Monies and Their Relatives* (Washington: Dumbarton Oaks Research Library and Collection, 1990).
28. Hosler, Lechtman, and Holm, *Axe-Monies and Their Relatives*, 3, 17.
29. George E. Stuart, Ph.D., "Riddle of the Glyphs," *National Geographic*, Dec. 1975; Foundation for the Advancement of Mesoamerican Studies, Inc., "The Madrid Codex," http://www.famsi.org/mayawriting/codices/madrid.html (accessed Sept. 19, 2008); Taxay, *Money of the American Indians*, 2.
30. Hosler, Lechtman, and Holm, *Axe-Monies and Their Relatives*, 39.
31. Alberto Francisco Pradeau, *Numismatic History of Mexico From the Pre-Columbian Epoch to 1823* (Los Angeles: A. F. Pradeau, 1938), 14.
32. Ibid., 14–18.
33. *Encyclopædia Britannica*, 14th ed., revised, s.v. "Chinese Bronze"; A. Terrien de Lacouperie, *Catalogue of Chinese Coins From the VIIth Cent. BC, to AD 621, Including the Series in the British Museum* (London: Trustees of the British Museum, 1892), ix, xxi; Qian Jiaju, *History of Chinese Currency*, 2.
34. Qian Jiaju, *History of Chinese Currency*, 2–3; Dai Zhiqiang and Zhou Weirong, "China,"*A Survey of Numismatic Research 1990–1995* (Berlin: International Association of Professional Numismatists, 1997), 793–794; Dai Zhiqiang and Helen Wang, "Numismatic Studies in China," *A Survey of Numismatic Research 1996–2001* (Madrid, International Association of Professional Numismatists, 2003), 695–696.
35. Shanghai Museum, *Coins in the Collection of the Shanghai Museum: Coins of the Pre-Qin Dynasties* [text in Chinese] (Shanghai: Shanghai Calligraphy & Painting Publishing House, 1994).
36. Qian Jiaju, *History of Chinese Currency*, 11; J.A. Brudin, *Coins of Wang Mang*, repr. from *The Numismatist*, 1963, 1–7.
37. Terrien de Lacouperie, *Chinese Coins*, xi–xii, 213.
38. Wang Yu-Ch'uan, *Early Chinese Coinage* (New York: The American Numismatic Society [Numismatic Notes and Monographs No. 122], 1951), 8–21, 144–179, pl. XXVII–L; Daxi, *Zhong Guo Li Dai Hou Xi (The Shanghai Encyclopedia)*, vol. 1 (Shanghai: Shanghai Numismatic Society and Shanghai Museum, 1988); Dai Zhiqiang and Helen Wang, "Numismatic Studies in China," 696–700; Dai Zhiqiang and Zhou Weirong, "China," 792–793; Brudin, *Coins of Wang Mang*, 8–9.
39. Einzig, *Primitive Money*, 152; Quiggin, *Primitive Money*, 98; Pitt Rivers Museum, "Uganda, Native-made iron hoe-blade, large form used only for bride purchase, Online Catalogue, no. 1923.23.12."
40. Sergei L. Solovyov, "Monetary circulation and the political history of archaic Borysthenes." *Ancient Civilizations from Scythia to Siberia* 12:1 (July 2006), abstract; Mihaela Manucu-Adamesteanu, "[The arrowhead money hoard from Vişina-Jurilovca, Tulcea County]," *SCN*, vol. 8 (1984), abstract; *Classical Numismatic Review*, vol. 18, No. 2 (1993 Second Quarter), "Specials—From Barter to Coinage;" author's collection.
41. Quiggin, *Primitive Money*, 142–143.
42. Arthur Woodward, *Indian Trade Goods* (Portland: Oregon Archaeological Society, 1965), 20–21, 27; Opitz, *Traditional Money*, 152–154; Hudson's Bay Company (HBC), "Our History: Business: Fur Trade: Standard of Trade," http://www.hbc.com/hbcheritage/history/business/fur/standardtrade.asp (accessed Oct. 1, 2008).
43. Einzig, *Primitive Money*, 165.

44. Crosby, *Early Coins*, 26.
45. Woodward, *Indian Trade Goods*, 16.
46. *History of Allegan and Barry counties, Michigan, with Illustrations and Biographical Sketches of their prominent men and pioneers* (Philadelphia: D.W. Ensign & Co., 1880), 148–149.
47. Opitz, *Traditional Money*, 270–271.
48. Einzig, *Primitive Money*, 91.
49. Opitz, *Traditional Money*, 250, 270–271, 395.
50. Sam Vulum, "Bride Price Still Very Much Alive in PNG," *Pacific Magazine* Dec. 1, 2002, http://www.pacificmagazine.net/issue/2002/12/01/bride-price-still-very-much-alive-in-png (accessed Sept. 30, 2008); Patricia May and Margaret Tuckson, *The Traditional Pottery of Papua New Guinea* (Honolulu: University of Hawai'i Press, 2000), 131, 151.
51. Opitz, *Traditional Money*, 271–272.
52. William Stanley Jevons, *Money and the Mechanism of Exchange* (New York: D. Appleton and Co., 1876 ed.), chap. IV., http://www.econlib.org/LIBRARY/YPDBooks/Jevons/jvnMME.html (accessed Sept. 30, 2008).
53. Einzig, *Primitive Money*, 116.
54. Ibid., *Primitive Money*, 278.
55. D.M. Metcalf, *Coinage in South-Eastern Europe 820–1396* (London: Royal Numismatic Society, 1979), 175.
56. Einzig, *Primitive Money*, 281, 116.
57. *Connecticut Gazette*, vol. XXVI, no. 1322 (Mar. 13, 1789).
58. Einzig, *Primitive Money*, 109, 116, 281, 299, 172, 295, 279–280.
59. Arthur Samet, *Pictorial Encyclopedia of Furs* (New York: Arthur Samet, 1950), 236–238; Einzig, *Primitive Money*, 385.
60. Peter Stockham, ed., *Little Book of Early American Crafts & Trades* (New York: Dover Publications, Inc., 1976), 25.
61. Einzig, *Primitive Money*, 172.
62. Taxay, *Money of the American Indians*, 94.
63. *The Canadian Encyclopedia*, "Made Beaver," http://thecanadianencyclopedia.com/index.cfm?PgNm=TCE&Params=A1ARTA0005026, (accessed Oct. 1, 2008); Einzig, *Primitive Money*, 174–175.
64. Joseph Barlow Felt, *Historical Account of Massachusetts Currency* (Boston: Perkins and Marvin, 1839; repr. New York: Burt Franklin, 1967), 15; Taxay, *Money of the American Indians*, 145.
65. *Connecticut Gazette*.
66. Einzig, *Primitive Money*, 299.
67. Conrad Weiser, *Pennsylvania Provincial Council Minutes*, Colonial Records, vol. V (Harrisburg: Theo. Fenn & Co., 1851), 348–358.
68. Samuel W. Johnson Jr., "My Price Was 107 Bucks or Dollars," Illinois Numismatic Association *Coin Digest* (Winter 1983), 9–16.
69. John Haywood, *Civil and Political History of Tennessee* (Nashville: W.H. Haywood, 1891), 150.
70. Henry Howe, *Historical Collections of Ohio*, vol. II. (Norwalk: The State of Ohio, 1896), 459.
71. Curtis, "Media of Exchange," 159.
72. Einzig, *Primitive Money*, 256–257.
73. Dai Zhiqiang and Yao Shuomin, "China," *A Survey of Numismatic Research 1985–1990* (Brussels: International Association of Professional Numismatists, 1991), 705.
74. Peter Spufford, *Money and Its Use in Medieval Europe* (Cambridge: Cambridge University Press, 1988), 71–72, 79; Dmitrij Mishin, "Ibrahim Ibn-Ya'qub At-Turtushi's Account of the Slavs from the Middle of the Tenth Century," M.A. thesis (chapter), *Annual of Medieval Studies at the CEU 1994–1995* (Budapest: Department of Medieval Studies, Central European University, 1996), 65, 184–199.
75. Einzig, *Primitive Money*, 273.
76. Ibid., 270.
77. E.B. Banning and L.A. Pavlish, "Observations on Primitive Money," *The Numismatist* 93:10 (Oct. 1980), 2432–2435; Michael D. Coe, *Mexico*, 3rd ed. (New York: Thames and Hudson, 1984), 149, 154, 158–159; Pradeau, *Numismatic History of Mexico*, 9–16; Friar Diego de Landa (1566) *Yucatan Before and After the Conquest*, trans. William Gates (New York: Dover, 1978), 37.
78. Taxay, *Money of the American Indians*, 29.
79. Coe, *Mexico*, 158.
80. Taxay, *Money of the American Indians*, 96–98.

81. Ibid., 100.
82. *Encyclopædia Britannica*, 14th ed., revised, s.v. "Potlatch."
83. Einzig, *Primitive Money*, 122, 138–140, 152–153, 164, 167–168.
84. Opitz, *Traditional Money*, 109–111.
85. W.P. Tisdel, Letter dated June 29, 1885, in United States Department of State, *Papers Relating to the Foreign Relations of the United States Transmitted to Congress With the Annual Message of the President, Dec. 8, 1885* (Washington: Government Printing Office, 1886), 305; Col. Phares O. Sigler, "The Primitive Money of Africa. Chapter III. Cloth," *The Numismatist* 65:8 (Aug. 1952), 782–784; Einzig, *Primitive Money*, 122, 128, 131, 134, 136–140, 145–146, 154–156, 164–165, 167–168.
86. Einzig, *Primitive Money*, 100–102; Opitz, *Traditional Money*, 161–162.
87. Lilian A. Bell, *Papyrus, Tapa, Amate & Rice Paper: Papermaking in Africa, the Pacific, Latin America & Southeast Asia* (McMinnville, Oregon: Liliaceae Press, 1983), 41, 74; Judith Cameron, "Trans-oceanic transfer of bark-cloth technology from South China—Southeast Asia to Mesoamerica?" 204, http://epress.anu.edu.au/terra_australis/ta29/pdf/ch13.pdf (accessed Oct. 2, 2008); Tsien Tsuen-Hsuin, *Science & Civilisation in China*, vol. V: 1, ed. Joseph Needham (Cambridge: Cambridge University Press, 1985), 110.
88. Simon Kooijman, "Tapa in Polynesia," *Bishop Museum Bulletin* 234 (1972), 2–5, Table G, 193.
89. Margaret Mead, *Coming of Age in Samoa* (New York: The New American Library, 1949) (reprint of 1928 ed.), 161.
90. Quiggin, *Primitive Money*, 111.
91. Gale Scott Troxler, *Fijian Masi: A Traditional Art Form*, (Greensboro, North Carolina: The Piedmont Press, 1971), 16; Quiggin, *Primitive Money*, 134.
92. Maxine J. Tamahori, "Cultural Change in Tongan Bark-Cloth Manufacture," (master's thesis, University of Auckland, 1963), 223–229.
93. Willowdean Chatterson Handy, "Tattooing in the Marquesas," *Bishop Museum Bulletin* 1 (1922), 3.
94. Adel Allouche, *Mamluk Economics, A Study and Translation of Al-Maqrīzī's Ighathah* (Salt Lake City: University of Utah Press, 1994), 69.
95. Einzig, *Primitive Money*, 272–273.
96. Information supplied by local guide at Mošćenice, Croatia, June 14, 2005.
97. Einzig, *Primitive Money*, 310.
98. Marco Polo, *The Travels of Marco Polo*, ed. Ernest Rhys (London and New York: J. M. Dent & Sons, E. P. Dutton & Co., 1908, repr. 1936), 240–242.
99. Allen M. Blair, *A World of Money From the Earliest Times: A Concise Non-Eurocentric History of the World's Native Currencies*, 2nd ed. (Alexandria, MN: Northcountry Publishing Co., 1997), 57; Einzig, *Primitive Money*, 104; Quiggin, *Primitive Money*, 201–202.
100. Howland Wood, *The Coinage of Ethiopia*, (New York: Wayte Raymond, Inc., 1937), 3; Quiggin, *Primitive Money*, 51–55.
101. Einzig, *Primitive Money*, 123; Opitz, *Traditional Money*, 289–290.
102. William Atherton Du Puy, "The Geography of Money," *National Geographic* 52:6 (Dec. 1927), 746.
103. Tim Sullivan, untitled Associated Press story datelined Taoudenni, Mali, Jan. 7, 2001.
104. Espadim Coleccionismo, "O SAL em ANGOLA," hi5 message board posting, Mar. 21, 2008, http://hi5.com/friend/group/1934520—10841596—Espadim—O%2BSAL%2Bem%2BANGOLA—topic-html (accessed Oct. 4, 2008); Quiggin, *Primitive Money*, 54.
105. Opitz, *Traditional Money*, 291; Felicia Ekejiuba, "Currency Instability and Social Payments Among the Igbo of Eastern Nigeria," in *Money Matters: Instability, Values and Social Payments in the Modern History of West African Communities*, ed. Jane Guyer, (Portsmouth, NH: Heinemann, 1995), 136–137; Quiggin, *Primitive Money*, 84–85.
106. Paul M. Dillingham, "Odd and Curious List #3" (ca. 1969), 2; "List Number 6" (1970), 1; "Odd, Curious and Primitive Money" advertisement, AP26, *World Coins* 11:6 (June, 1974), 1189; "List #16" (ca. 1976), 3; "List #17" (ca. 1977), 3 and figure.
107. Mark Kurlansky, *Salt: A World History* (New York: Penguin Books, 2002), 205.
108. Taxay, *Money of the American Indians*, 58.
109. Quiggin, *Primitive Money*, 257–259; Opitz, *Traditional Money*, 292–293.
110. *Encyclopædia Britannica*, 14th ed., revised, "Pepper."
111. Edward Gibbon, *The Decline and Fall of the Roman Empire*, vol. 2, ed. Oliphant Smeaton (New York: The Modern Library [Random House], n.d. [ca. 1970 printing]), 130, 155.

112. Einzig, *Primitive Money*, 266, footnote 10.
113. Podał Stefan Dybowski, "Bolesław the Pious and the "Kalisz Statute" for the Jews of the Year 1264," *Gazeta Kaliska*, 2 czerwca 1929 roku, http://www.info.kalisz.pl/statut/index.html (accessed Oct. 5, 2008).
114. Donald B. Woodward and Marc A. Rose, *A Primer of Money* (New York and London: Whittlesey House, 1932), pl. facing 208.
115. Spufford, *Medieval Europe*, 98; Einzig, *Primitive Money*, 268.
116. Einzig, *Primitive Money*, 100.
117. Central Queensland University, School of Humanities, Dept. of History, "52148: Imperialism and Commodities: Spices," http://www.ahs.cqu.edu.au/humanities/history/52148/modules /imperial_commoditiesZ.html (accessed June 18, 2007); Peter N. Stearns, general ed., *The Encyclopedia of World History*, 6th ed. (Houghton Mifflin Company, 2001); http://www.bartleby.com /67/841.html (accessed Sept. 19, 2008).
118. Sophie D. Coe and Michael D. Coe, *The True History of Chocolate* (New York: Thames & Hudson, 2000), 50; Gonzalo Fernández de Oviedo y Valdés, *Historia general y natural de las Indias: Part 1 (1535)*, in HTML at Early Modern Spain, King's College London: Libro VIII, Capítulo XXX, http://www.ems.kcl.ac.uk/content/etext/e026.html (accessed Oct. 5, 2008).
119. Coe and Coe, *History of Chocolate*, 35–61.
120. Ibid., 85.
121. Pradeau, *Numismatic History of Mexico*, 10–11.
122. Coe and Coe, *History of Chocolate*, 84; John Kellermeier, "Aztec Tribute Record Numerals," http://www.tacomacc.edu/home/jkellerm/MATH106/EthnomathematicsText/Chapter2/Aztec Numerals.htm (accessed Oct. 5, 2008); Miguel L. Muñoz, "Mexico 1536: Prima Numisma America," *The Numismatist*, May 1966, 564.
123. Oviedo y Valdés, *Historia general*.
124. Coe and Coe, *History of Chocolate*, 98–99.
125. Pradeau, *Numismatic History of Mexico*, 12.
126. Oviedo y Valdés, *Historia general*.
127. Hubert Howe Bancroft, *The Works of Hubert Howe Bancroft*, vol. I, *The Native Races. Wild Tribes* (San Francisco: A. L. Bancroft & Co., 1883), 699–700.
128. Einzig, *Primitive Money*, 183; B. E. Dahlgren, *Cacao* (Chicago: Field Museum of Natural History, 1923), 6.
129. Lee F. Hewitt, "From the Editor," *The Numismatic Scrapbook Magazine* 11 (Nov. 15, 1945), 1141.
130. United Press International, "Peru uses candy as coinage," *Chicago Tribune* June 29, 1975: sect. 1, 22.
131. Associated Press, "Sticks of Gum Used As Coins in Mexico," Feb. 20, 1958 (unidentified clipping).
132. *Numismatic News Weekly*, "Italy Experiences 10 Lire Shortage," Jan. 1, 1974, 12; *Moneysworth*, "Four Course Currency." Jan. 17, 1977, 3; "Italians get coins once more," *Coin World*, Jan. 18, 1978, 56.
133. Robert D. Leonard Jr., "Small-Change Substitutes in Kyrgyzstan, 1999," *International Primitive Money Society Newsletter* [40] (Feb., 2000), n.p.
134. "India addresses coin shortage—maybe," *World Coin News*, Sept. 2008, 20.
135. Saul Bellus, "Cardboard Cent of Boise, Idaho," *The Numismatist*, Dec. 1947, 855.
136. *Numismatic News*, Feb. 3, 1979, 3, quoting Carol Barnes, a staff writer for the *Amarillo Globe-News*.
137. M. Huc, *Travels in Tartary, Thibet and China During the Years 1844-5-6*, trans. W. Hazlitt (Chicago: The Open Court Publishing Company, 1900), 71.
138. Ken Bressett, "Tea Money of China," *International Primitive Money Society Newsletter* 44 (Aug. 2001); Wolfgang Bertsch, "The Use of Tea Bricks as Currency Among the Tibetans," *International Primitive Money Society Newsletter* 54 (Aug. 2006), 55 (Mar. 2007).
139. Sir Alan Burns, *History of Nigeria*, 5th ed. (London: George Allen and Unwin Ltd., 1955), 230.
140. Einzig, *Primitive Money*, 149–150.
141. Ekejiuba, "Currency Instability," 149.
142. "Cash is good, but vodka is better in Russia," *Coin World*, Oct. 19, 1998, 86.
143. "Vodka," *Coin World*, Feb. 17, 1992, 56.
144. Frederick Kempe, "Quid Pro Quo—Poles Survive Collapse of Currency by Using Own System of Barter," *The Wall Street Journal*, Oct. 23, 1981: 1, 1, 16.

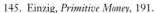

145. Einzig, *Primitive Money*, 191.

146. Kathleen Kouril, "Algeria's Hard Currency," *The Wall Street Journal*, Feb. 12, 1987: sect. 1, 20.

147. Louis E. Jordan, "Somer Islands 'Hogge Money' of 1616: The Historical Context," *The Colonial Newsletter* 43:2 (Aug. 2003; Serial No. 123), 2465–2493.

148. Einzig, *Primitive Money*, 290.

149. A. Hyatt Verrill, *Romantic and Historic Virginia* (New York: Dodd, Mead & Company, 1935), 39; George F. Willison, *Behold Virginia: The Fifth Crown* (New York: Harcourt, Brace and Co., 1952), 216–217.

150. Einzig, *Primitive Money*, 302.

151. Ibid., 91; Quiggin, *Primitive Money*, 109, 117, 127, 136 footnote 2; Opitz, *Traditional Money*, 352–354.

152. John Kenneth Galbraith, *Money: Whence It Came, Whence It Went* (Boston: Houghton Mifflin, 1975), 250–251.

153. Hewitt, *Numismatic Scrapbook Magazine*.

154. R.A. Radford, "The Economic Organization of a P.O.W. Camp," *Economica*, Nov. 1945: 189–201.

155. Einzig, *Primitive Money*, 309–310; Opitz, *Traditional Money*, 106.

156. Einzig, *Primitive Money*, 104.

157. Nguyen Kien, *Vietnam: 15 Years After the Liberation of Saigon* (Hanoi: Foreign Languages Publishing House, 1990), 27–39; "Foreign Cigarettes Banned," *Parade*, Nov. 30, 1980, 25; Nayan Chanda, "A last-minute rescue," *Far Eastern Economic Review*, Feb. 27, 1981, 28–30; Roger Thurow, "In Romania, Smoking A Kent Cigarette Is Like Burning Money," *The Wall Street Journal*, Jan. 3, 1986: sect. 1, 6.

158. Karen Elliott House and David Satter, "Unchanging Russia: In the Andropov Era, Soviet System Reverts Quickly to Old Ways," *The Wall Street Journal*, July 1, 1983, 1, 21.

159. Sandy Stuart, "Convicted of Murder, Weber Trying To Make The Most of Prison Life," *The Bernardsville News* (Bernardsville, NJ), Dec. 10, 1981, 1–2.

160. Quoted by Dr. Philip Carrigan, a member of the John Howard Association of Illinois, who attended a lecture there (personal communication, Oct. 16, 2006).

161. Blair, *World of Money*, 61–61; Karen Human Rights Group, "Brief Interviews Regarding Opium, Feb. 1, 1993," http://www.khrg.org/khrg93/93_02_01a.html (accessed Oct. 7, 2008); Emilie Astell, "Couple working to weaken opium's grip," *Worcestor Telegram & Gazette*, repr. by Poppies.org, http://www.poppies.org/2001/07/09/couple-working-to-weaken-opiums-grip/ (accessed Oct. 7, 2008).

162. Philip Shishkin and David Crawford, "Heavy Traffic—In Afghanistan, Heroin Trade Soars Despite U.S. Aid," *The Wall Street Journal*, Jan. 18, 2006, A1, A8.

163. Frank Swertlow, "Hollywood's Cocaine Connection, first of two parts," *TV Guide*, Feb. 28, 1981, 6–12.

164. Robert D. Leonard Jr., "The Use of Stamps as Money," *The Numismatist*, Nov. 1963, 1495–1503.

165. George B. Sloane, *Sloane's Column*, comp. by George T. Turner, (West Somerville: Bureau Issues Association, Inc., 1961), 156–157 (Dec. 14, 1935, May 30, 1953); Robert Chandler, "Part III. Gold as a Cumbersome Curmudgeonly Commodity 1849–1870." *The Brasher Bulletin*, Fall/Winter 2006, 12.

166. Robert D. Leonard Jr., "When Stamps Were Money," *The Numismatist*, Feb. 2002, 178–183, 235.

167. Leonard, "Use of Stamps"; Courtney L. Coffing, "Stamps Sub For Coins in Money Crises," *Numismatic Scrapbook Magazine*, 1730–1738; 36: 268–272, and 772–778 (Nov. 25, 1969; Feb. 25, 1970; June 25, 1970); Captain F. Pridmore, "The Emergency Currency Measures of Cyprus 1942–1943," *The Numismatic Circular*, Sept. 1967, 235–237; E. Jagger, "Use of Cyprus Postage Stamps for Currency" (Letter to the Editor), *The Holy Land Philatelist* 66/67 (Apr./May 1960), 1352.

168. Leonard, "When Stamps"; Leonard, "Use of Stamps," 1501–1502.

169. Courtney L. Coffing, "World Stamp Encasements Enhance Many Collections" (title varies), *The Numismatic Scrapbook Magazine* 35: 284–287, 456–461, 644–650, 810–815, 924–929, and 1068–1078; (Feb. 25, 1969; Mar. 25, 1969; Apr. 25, 1969; May 25, 1969; June 25, 1969; July 25, 1969).

Chapter 4

1. Abdeljalil Bouzouggar, Nick Barton, Marian Vanhaeren, et al., "82,000-year-old shell beads from North Africa and implications for the origins of modern human behavior" (abstr.), *Proceedings of the National Academy of Sciences of the United States of America*, June 4, 2007, http://www.pnas

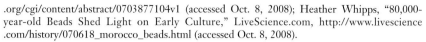

.org/cgi/content/abstract/0703877104v1 (accessed Oct. 8, 2008); Heather Whipps, "80,000-year-old Beads Shed Light on Early Culture," LiveScience.com, http://www.livescience.com/history/070618_morocco_beads.html (accessed Oct. 8, 2008).

2. Whipps, ibid.

3. V.N. Misra and Peter Bellwood, eds. *Recent Advances in Indo-Pacific Prehistory* (Leiden: Brill, 1985), 144.

4. Richard G. Klein, *Ice-Age Hunters of the Ukraine* (Chicago: The University of Chicago Press, 1973), 7, 17, 20, 72, 84–89.

5. Einzig, *Primitive Money*, 169; Quiggin, *Primitive Money*, 100, 107; The Online Guide to Namibia. "The people of Namibia: Information on ethnic groups." http://www.namibweb.com/people.html (accessed Oct. 8, 2008); Clive Cowley, "Clive Cowley's Journey into Namibia: Namibia guidebook #14." http://www.orusovo.com/guidebook/content2.htm (accessed Oct. 13, 2008).

6. Taxay, *Money of the American Indians*, 110.

7. Ibid., 110–136.

8. Ibid., 107–109.

9. Ibid., 65–68.

10. Quiggin, *Primitive Money*, 162–163; Einzig, *Primitive Money*, 68.

11. Einzig, *Primitive Money*, 68–69.

12. Opitz, *Traditional Money*, 51.

13. Taxay, *Money of the American Indians*, 37–40; Opitz, *Traditional Money*, 52.

14. Quiggin, *Primitive Money*, 249; Lois Sherr Dubin, *The History of Beads from 30,000 BC to the Present* (New York: Harry N. Abrams, Inc., 1987), 162, 167, 174; *Encyclopædia Britannica*, 14th ed., revised, s.v. "Japan"; Charles T. Keally, "Japanese Archaeology: Kofun Culture," Mar. 14, 2008, http://www.t-net.ne.jp/~keally/kofun.html (accessed Oct. 9, 2008); Miho Museum, "Agate Magatama." http://www.miho.or.jp/booth/html/artcon/00005285e.htm (accessed Oct. 9, 2008).

15. Polo, *Travels*, 239.

16. Dubin, *History of Beads*, 209.

17. Opitz, *Traditional Money*, 117; Dubin, *History of Beads*, 211.

18. Opitz, *Traditional Money*, 46–47; Peter Francis Jr., "Faience," Center for Bead Research, 2002. http://www.thebeadsite.com/BB-FA.html (accessed Oct. 12, 2008).

19. Einzig, *Primitive Money*, 53–56; Charles J. Opitz, *Traditional Money on Yap & Palau* (Ocala: First Impressions Printing, Inc., 2004), 2.

20. Quiggin, *Primitive Money*, 148–149; Nicholas J. Goetzfridt and Karen M. Peacock, *Micronesian Histories: An Analytical Bibliography and Guide to Interpretations* (Westport: Greenwood Press, 2002), 293, entry for Robert E. Ritzenthaler.

21. Opitz, *Yap & Palau*, 1–2, 6, 10; Goetzfridt and Peacock, *Micronesian Histories*, entry for Francesca K. Remengesau.

22. Einzig, *Primitive Money*, 53–55; Gerd Koch, "Geld in Ozeanien." Staatliche Museen Prußischer Kulturbesitz–Berlin, Museen für Völkerkunde: Abteilung Südsee 082 3 (1972).

23. Koch, ibid.; Peter E. Patacsil, "Classifying Traditional Palauan Money: Ethnomathematics Conveys Cultural Pride," *Calcoin News* Winter 2003, http://www.coinmail.com/CSNA/art031.htm (accessed Oct. 18, 2007); Opitz, *Yap & Palau*, 6.

24. Einzig, *Primitive Money*, 53.

25. The Venerable Beadle (pseud.), "The Bead Column: Making Chevron Beads by Lampworking," *Glass Line* 9:3 (Oct./Nov. 1995), citing G. Sarpellon, *Miniature Masterpieces: Mosaic Glass 1858 1924* (New York: Prestel Verlag, 1995), 17, http://www.glassline.net/guests/access/vol9/v9n3.html (accessed Oct. 11, 2008); Woodward, *Indian Trade Goods*, 9–10; The Bead Database, "Chevron Beads." http://bead-database.org/index.php?option=com_gallery2&Itemid=26&g2_itemId=1664 (accessed Oct. 11, 2008).

26. Dubin, *History of Beads*, 111–117, 346; Opitz, *Traditional Money*, 42.

27. Opitz, *Traditional Money*, 42–43; The Bead Database, "Chevron Beads"; Quiggin, *Primitive Money*, 261.

28. Dubin, *History of Beads*, 97, 274, 344; Opitz, *Traditional Money*, 46.

29. Dubin, *History of Beads*, 108–109, 258–259; Mary Elizabeth Good, *Guebert Site: an 18th-Century Historic Kaskaskia Indian Village in Randolph County, Illinois* (Wood River, Illinois: Central States Archaeological Societies, Inc., 1972), 100, 121–123; William C. Orchard, *Beads and Beadwork of the American Indians*, 2nd. ed. (New York: Museum of the American Indian / Heye Foundation, 1975), 102.

30. Peter Francis Jr., "The Aggrey Bead and its Namesakes," http://www.thebeadsite.com/BNAF -AGG.htm (accessed Oct. 12, 2008); Quiggin, *Primitive Money*, 37; Peter Francis Jr., "Beads," *Fustat Finds*, ed. Jere L. Bacharach (Cairo: The American University in Cairo Press, 2002), 16.
31. Steenie Harvey, "How to Profit From African Beads," *International Living*, Apr. 9, 2008, http://www.internationalliving.com/publications/Free-E-Letters/IL-Postcards/04-09-08-beads (accessed Oct. 12, 2008); Quiggin, *Primitive Money*, 37–39; Opitz, *Traditional Money*, 57; Dubin, *History of Beads*, 60, 111–112, Bead Chart 47, 55a–I, 65a–e, 76, 77a–c, 78a–b.
32. Dubin, *History of Beads*, 60, 112.
33. Quiggin, *Primitive Money*, 37; Einzig, *Primitive Money*, 154; H.A. Wieschhoff, "Primitive Money," *University Museum Bulletin*, Dec. 1945 (Philadelphia: The University Museum, University of Pennsylvania, 1945), 34.
34. Peter Francis Jr., "Chinese Glass Beads: New Evidence," http://www.thebeadsite.com/be02 -ch.htm (accessed Oct. 12, 2008); Johanna Hecht, "The Manila Galleon Trade (1565–1815)," The Metropolitan Museum of Art, Heilbrunn Timeline of Art History, http://www.metmuseum .org/toah/hd/mgtr/hd_mgtr.htm (accessed Oct. 12, 2008); Cloyd Sorensen, "The Enduring Intrigue of the Glass Trade Bead," *Arizona Highways* 47:7 (July 1971), 16, 19, 21–23, 28, 32, 34–37; Opitz, *Traditional Money*, 59.
35. Woodward, *Indian Trade Goods*, 14–15, 33–36; Dubin, *History of Beads*, 108.
36. David W. Griffiths & Kevin Robinson [corrected] with Melissa Darby, *Echachist: A Preliminary Archaeological Survey and Analysis with Ethnographic Notes Prepared for the Tla-O-Qui-Aht First Nation* (Tofino, BC: Tonquin Foundation, Sept. 2004), 6–7; Opitz, *Traditional Money*, 62.
37. Good, *Guebert Site*, 106, Color Plate 3; Opitz, *Traditional Money*, 62.
38. Scott Semans, "Trade Beads," http://www.coincoin.com/seXG.htm (accessed Oct. 12, 2008); Dubin, *History of Beads*, 109.
39. Peter Francis Jr., "Excavations at Arikamedu," http://www.thebeadsite.com/UNI-ARK.html (accessed Oct. 13, 2008); Peter Francis Jr., "Indo-Pacific Beads," http://www.thebeadsite .com/REC-OGL.html (accessed Oct. 13, 2008); Opitz, *Traditional Money*, 52; Dubin, *History of Beads*, 195.
40. Francis, "Indo-Pacific Beads"; Opitz, *Traditional Money*, 52; Dubin, *History of Beads*, 184.
41. Dubin, *History of Beads*, 128; Peter Robertshaw, Marilee Wood, Rachel Popelka-Filcoff, and Michael Glascock, "Glass Beads of Southern Africa and Indian Ocean Trading Networks," http://cohesion.rice.edu/CentersAndInst/SAFA/emplibrary/Robertshaw,P.etalSafa2006.pdf (accessed Oct. 13, 2008).
42. Shinnie, *Ancient African Kingdoms*, 153; Graham Connah, *African Civilizations* (Cambridge: Cambridge University Press, 1987), 189–190, 211; Dubin, *History of Beads*, 132.
43. C.R. Boxer and Carlos de Azevedo, *Fort Jesus and the Portuguese in Mombasa 1593–1729* (London: Hollis & Carter, 1960), 14.
44. Francis, "Indo-Pacific Beads"; Opitz, *Traditional Money*, 58; Dubin, *History of Beads*, 226.
45. Richard Hobbs, *Treasure: Finding Our Past* (London: The British Museum Press, 2003), 102–103 (footnote 5), 152.
46. Chris Rudd, "Forged ring money deceives collectors," *World Coin News* Sept. 2006, 49–50.
47. Ernest F. Cooke, "Jokla—Navaho Earrings," *The Numismatist* 79:5 (May 1966): 588–590; John Adair, *The Navajo and Pueblo Silversmiths* (Norman, University of Oklahoma Press, 1944).
48. Colchester Treasure Hunting and Metal Detecting, "Celtic Gold Torcs—The Great Torc from Snettisham," http://www.colchestertreasurehunting.co.uk/torcs.htm (accessed Oct. 13, 2008).
49. Nghiêm Van Đảng, Chu Thái Són, and Lúu Hùng, *Ethnic Minorities in Vietnam* (Hanoi: The Gioi Publishers, 1993); Harry A. Franck, *East of Siam* (New York: The Century Co., 1926), 269–273.
50. Quiggin, *Primitive Money*, 75–76; Opitz, *Traditional Money*, 42; Angela Fisher, *Africa Adorned* (New York: Harry N. Abrams, Inc., 1984), 84–85.
51. Quiggin, *Primitive Money*, 16–17, 120–123, 160–162, 174–175, 180–183; Einzig, *Primitive Money*, 67, 79–83.
52. Sven-Olof Johansson, *Nigerian Currencies: Manillas Cowries and Others*, 2nd. ed. (Norrköping, 1967), 16, 62–65; Fisher, *Africa Adorned*, 88–89; P. Amaury Talbot, *The Peoples of Southern Nigeria* (Oxford: Oxford University Press, 1926), 878.
53. Quiggin, *Primitive Money*, 76; Fisher, ibid.; Opitz, *Traditional Money*, 276–279.
54. Quiggin, *Primitive Money*, 25–36; Banning and Pavlish, "Observations on Primitive Money," 2430; A.S. Kenyon, "The Cowrie Shell In Primitive Currency," *The Numismatist* 54:5 (May 1941), 340–342; Dubin, *History of Beads*, 230; Henry C. Koerper and Nancy Whitney-Desautels, "A

Cowry Shell Artifact from Bolsa Chica: An Example of Prehistoric Exchange," *Pacific Coast Archaeological Society Quarterly* 35:2–3 (Spring and Summer 1999), 84, www.pcas.org/Vol35N23 /3523Koerper2.pdf (accessed Oct. 14, 2008).

55. Dai Zhiqiang and Zhou Weirong, "China," 791; Qian Jiaju, *History of Chinese Currency*, 1.
56. Arthur Braddan Coole, *Coins in China's History*, 4th ed. (Mission, Kansas: Arthur B. Coole, 1965), 10; Banning and Pavlish, "Observations on Primitive Money," 2430; David Crook et al (Beijing Foreign Language Institute), *A Chinese-English Dictionary* (Shangwu Yinshuguan [Chubanshe] China, 1988), 26, 286, 305.
57. Terrien de Lacouperie, *Chinese Coins*, x.
58. Quiggin, *Primitive Money*, 224; Terrien de Lacouperie, *Chinese Coins*, xiv–xv; Polo, *Travels*, 243–245.
59. Quiggin, *Primitive Money*, 28–29; Einzig, *Primitive Money*, 102–103.
60. Quiggin, *Primitive Money*, 29, 98–100.
61. Einzig, *Primitive Money*, 134.
62. Johansson, *Nigerian Currencies*, 28–35.
63. Quiggin, *Primitive Money*, 35, 178; Walter Thompson, "Money Cowry," *The Numismatic Scrapbook Magazine* 28:5 (May 1962), 1300–1302.
64. Taxay, *Money of the American Indians*, 74–77.
65. Ibid., 88; Edward T. Stevens, "On the Dentalium Shell and Shell-Money," *The Technologist* Mar. 1, 1865, 355–356.
66. [Richard Alsop], *A Narrative of the Adventures and Sufferings, of John R. Jewitt; only survivor of the crew of the Ship Boston, during a captivity of nearly three years among the savages of Nootka Sound* (Middletown: Loomis & Richards, 1815), 74–76.
67. Ibid.; Taxay, *Money of the American Indians*, 83–85.
68. Quiggin, *Primitive Money*, 141–144.
69. Opitz, *Traditional Money*, 176–178.
70. Quiggin, *Primitive Money*, 126–127; Einzig, *Primitive Money*, 176; Stuart Mosher, "The Story of Money as Told by the Knox Collection," *Bulletin of the Buffalo Society of Natural Sciences* 17:2, 1936, 37–39.
71. Einzig, *Primitive Money*, 69; Yaroslav Trofimov, "Shrinking Dollar Meets Its Match in Dolphin Teeth," *The Wall Street Journal* Apr. 30, 2008, A1, A13.
72. Quiggin, *Primitive Money*, 125–126; Einzig, *Primitive Money*, 90; Opitz, *Traditional Money*, 87–88.
73. Einzig, *Primitive Money*, 44; Opitz, *Traditional Money*, 378–379.
74. Quiggin, *Primitive Money*, 126, 128; Radford Stearns, "Tooth Money: A Great Way to Fill the Holes in Your Collection," *The Numismatist* 100:2 (Feb. 1987), 270; Pitt Rivers Museum, "Fiji currency, Online Catalogue, no. 1884.99.15."
75. Mosher, *Story of Money*, 74.
76. Pitt Rivers Museum, "Oceania—Feather string, Vanuatu," http://www.prm.ox.ac.uk/LGweb /feathers/1920_100_376.htm (accessed Oct. 16, 2008); Quiggin, *Primitive Money*, 135; Opitz, *Traditional Money*, 144.

Chapter 5

1. "Shell rings found in Middle East graves may be primitive money," *Coin World*, Sept. 25, 1995, 67.
2. Quiggin, *Primitive Money*, 120–122.
3. Ibid., 144, 164; Einzig, *Primitive Money*, 54, 58; Opitz, *Traditional Money*, 360; Opitz, *Yap & Palau*, 18.
4. Quiggin, *Primitive Money*, 167–168.
5. Comte de Widranges, "Ancient Gaulish Money. Rings and Wheels," *Archaeologia Cambrensis* Jan. 1861, 213–230; Gerloff, Hansen, and Oehler, *Bronzezeit aus Frankreich*, Taf. 33–35; Frascatius Ancients, eBay auction May 15, 2008, and others (found in large quantities in the Eastern Balkans, and offered in lots of 10 and 100); Quiggin, *Primitive Money*, 276.
6. Jiří Sejbal, *Dějiny Peněz Na Moravě* (Brno: Blok, 1979), tab. I.
7. Quiggin, *Primitive Money*, 280–281, pl. 28, 1.
8. L.A. Saryan, "Ring money or just rings," *World Coin News* 16:24 (June 13, 1989), 16–19.
9. Observed by author, 1981. Two preserved in author's collection.
10. The British Museum, "Brass manilla (bracelet)," http://www.britishmuseum.org/explore /highlights/highlight_objects/aoa/b/brass_manilla_bracelet.aspx (accessed Oct. 17, 2008); Williams, *Money: A History*, 198, Fig. 288a.

11. Eugenia W. Herbert, *Red Gold of Africa*, (Madison: The University of Wisconsin Press, 1984), 113–121.
12. Herbert, *Red Gold of Africa*, 128.
13. Ivana Elbl, "Bruges or Antwerp? Some Factors Behind the Relocation of the Portuguese Crown Factory," paper delivered at 29th International Congress of Medieval Studies, May 6, 1994; Herbert, *Red Gold of Africa*, 125–126.
14. A.F.C. Ryder, *Benin and the Europeans 1485–1897* (London: Longmans, 1969), 40; Paula Girshick Ben-Amos, *The Art of Benin*, 2nd ed. (London: British Museum Press, 1995), 37, 40–42; Read & Dalton, *Antiquities from the City of Benin, etc. in the British Museum* (New York: Hacker Art Books, 1973, reprint of 1899 ed.), 3–4, 17, 27, pl. XII, XIII, XVI, XXI; Candice Goucher, Jehanne Teilhet, Kent R. Wilson, and Tsaihwa J. Chow, "Lead Isotope Analyses and Possible Metal Sources for Nigerian 'Bronzes,'" *Advances in Chemistry* 171, 278–292; Herbert, *Red Gold of Africa*, 126; Elbl, "Briges or Antwerp?"
15. Peter Francis Jr., "Manilla," The Center for Bead Research, 1998, http://www.thebeadsite.com /BNKMM001.html (accessed Oct. 18, 2008).
16. Herbert, *Red Gold of Africa*, 129, 153; P.E.H. Hair, Adam Jones, and Robin Law, *Barbot on Guinea, The Writings of Jean Barbot on West Africa 1678–1712* (London: The Hakluyt Society, 1992), 219, 303–304; E. Zay, *Histoire Monétaire des Colonies Françaises* (Paris: Typographie de J. Montorier, 1892), 246–248.
17. Col. Phares O. Sigler, "Strange Money of the World: Ring Money," *The Numismatist* 70:2, 130 (Feb. 1957); Scott Semans, "Manilla: Money of the Slave Trade," Seattle: Scott Semans Info Sheet 24, n.d. (1997?).
18. Herbert, *Red Gold of Africa*, 126, 129, 132.
19. Ibid., 136, 149–150; R.F.A. Grey, "Manillas," *The Nigerian Field* 16:2 (Apr. 1951), 54; Quiggin, *Primitive Money*, 89–90.
20. P. Amaury Talbot, *The Peoples of Southern Nigeria* (Oxford: Oxford University Press, 1926), 875–876.
21. P. Amaury Talbot, *Tribes of the Niger Delta* (London: Frank Cass & Co., Ltd., 1967, reprint of 1932 ed.), 281–282.
22. Walter Ibekwe Ofonagoro, *The Currency Revolution in Southern Nigeria 1880–1948*, African Studies Center, UCLA, Occasional Paper No. 14, July 1976, 18–20; United Africa Co. Ltd. [Bill Hallet], "The Manilla Problem," *Statistical & Economical Review*, No. 3, 1949, 44–56; O.O. Amogu, "The Introduction Into and Withdrawal of Manillas from the 'Oil Rivers' as Seen in Ndoki District," *Nigeria* 38 (1952), 139; Grey, "Manillas," 61–63.
23. Ofonagoro, *Currency Revolution*, 31.
24. Amogu, "Ndoki District," 136, 139; Ekpo Eyo, *Nigeria and the Evolution of Money* (Lagos: Central Bank of Nigeria in association with The Federal Department of Antiquities, 1979), 61; Grey, "Manillas," 65–66; Cribb, *Cowrie Shells to Credit Cards*, 32; Herbert, *Red Gold of Africa*, 220; Johansson, *Nigerian Currencies*, 19–20; Sven-Olof Johansson, *Nigerian Primitive Currency Values, with supplement to Nigerian Currencies*, Beirut: Ghassan Ka'war, 1968, 7–8.
25. Andrews, "Private Tomb"; Goede and Hirst, "Tomb of Benia"; Cribb, *Cowrie Shells to Credit Cards*, 21.
26. Anthony John Arkell, *A History of the Sudan From the Earliest Times to 1821*, 2nd ed. (London: University of London, Athlone Press, 1961), 107; Lt. Col. Count Gleichen, *The Anglo-Egyptian Sudan*, vol. I (London: His Majesty's Stationery Office, 1905), 120; N. du Quesne Bird, "Sudanese Ring Money in the Second Quarter of the 19th Century," *The Numismatic Circular* 82:11 (Nov. 1974), 437–438.
27. Robert P. Skinner, "Commerce in Abyssinia: A Report from the American Consul General at Marseilles," *New York Times*, Mar. 30, 1902, 9.
28. Howland Wood, *The Gampola Larin Hoard* (New York: The American Numismatic Society, 1934).
29. Stephen Album, *A Checklist of Islamic Coins*, 2nd. ed. (Santa Rosa: Stephen Album, 1998), 127–129.
30. Michael Mitchiner, *Oriental Coins and Their Values: The World of Islam* (London: Hawkins Publications, 1977), 313–316; Quiggin, *Primitive Money*, 267.
31. Le May, *Coinage of Siam*, 10–16, 72–85, 138–142; Ulrich Guehler, "Further Studies of Old Thai Coins," *Journal of the Siam Society* 35:2 (1944), 69–70 (repr. in *Siamese Coins and Tokens*, 1977, 231–232).
32. Opitz, *Traditional Money*, 92–97; Le May, *Coinage of Siam*, 63–65, 151–152.
33. Opitz, *Traditional Money*, 171.

34. Ibid., 199–200; Le May, *Coinage of Siam*, 12–13, 139; Ulrich Guehler, "Notes on Old Siamese Coins." *Journal of the Siam Society* 37:1 (1948), 14, 20–21 (repr. in *Siamese Coins and Tokens*, 1977, 292, 298–299); Mosher, *Story of Money*, 32, 76.
35. Dr. S.P. Martini, "The Shell Coins of North Siam," *The Coin Collectors Journal* 3:11 (Feb. 1937), 243–245; Le May, *Coinage of Siam*, 123–124, 198; Opitz, *Traditional Money*, 250, 354–355.
36. J. Nenquin, "The Congo, Rwanda, and Burundi," *The African Iron Age*, ed. P. L. Shinnie (Oxford: Clarendon Press, 1971), 197–198, 214; Herbert, *Red Gold of Africa*, 186–190.
37. Quiggin, *Primitive Money*, 77–79; Opitz, *Traditional Money*, 124.
38. Quiggin, *Primitive Money*, 76–77; Connah, *African Civilizations*, 116; Mosher, *Story of Money*, 29.
39. Einzig, *Primitive Money*, 160–161.
40. Ibid., 161; Joseph Conrad, *Heart of Darkness*.
41. Quiggin, *Primitive Money*, 66–68; Opitz, *Traditional Money*, 89.
42. Qian Jiaju, *History of Chinese Currency*, 7; Bruce W. Smith, "Ch'u State Coinage" (handout from program on early Chinese money, Chicago Coin Club, August 13, 1997); Terrien de Lacouperie, *Chinese Coins*, xii–xiii, 300; Quiggin, *Primitive Money*, 225–227.
43. Col. Phares O. Sigler, "Strange Money of the World," repr. from *The Numismatist*, 1962, 4; Opitz, *Traditional Money*, 145, 352; Coole, *Coins in China's History*, 32; Bruce Smith (reported by Carl Wolf), "Primitive Money of Ancient China—Arguments and Evidence," program delivered at meeting of International Primitive Money Society, *International Primitive Money Society Newsletter* 43 (Feb. 2001), n.p.
44. Quiggin, *Primitive Money*, 253–256; William Shaw and Mohd. Kassim Haji Ali, *Coins of North Malaya* (Kuala Lumpur: Muzium Negara, 1971), 17–18.
45. Quiggin, *Primitive Money*, 252–254.
46. Sigler, *Strange Money* (1962), 11; Mitchiner, *Oriental Coins*, 466; Williams, *Money: A History*, 133; Quiggin, *Primitive Money*, 254.
47. The Bead Museum, "Courtship, Wedding and Marriage Beads: Mamuli," Arizona State Library, Arizona Memory Project, http://azmemory.lib.az.us/cdm4/colln_dir.php (search function accessed Oct. 22, 2008); The Metropolitan Museum of Art, "Ear Ornament or Pendant (Mamuli) [Kanatangu district, eastern Sumba Island, Nusa Tenggara, Indonesia] (1990.335.4)," *Heilbrunn Timeline of Art History*, 2000, http://www.metmuseum.org/TOAH/ho/10/sse/ho_1990.335.4.htm (accessed Oct. 22, 2008); Northern Territory Government, Australia, "Ritual Jewelry," Museums and Art Galleries of the Northern Territory, virtual exhibitions, Southeast Asia Link Gallery, http://www.nt.gov.au/nreta/museums/virtual/seagallery/gallery/ritual.html (accessed Oct. 22, 2008); B. Rabus (Stephen Bleeg, trans.), "Mamuli—Objects of Value From Sumba," International Primitive Money Society *Newsletter* 32 (July 1995), n.p.
48. Einzig, *Primitive Money*, 96 (Einzig appears to have supposed that kettledrums and gongs were two different objects, instead of two names for the same object); Quiggin, *Primitive Money*, 267–270, pl. 25; Opitz, *Traditional Money*, 226–227.
49. August Johan Bernet Kempers, *The Kettledrums of Southeast Asia: A Bronze Age world and its aftermath* (Rotterdam: A.A. Balkema, 1988); Opitz, *Traditional Money*, 226.
50. Einzig, *Primitive Money*, 96–97; Opitz, *Traditional Money*, 226–227.
51. Einzig, *Primitive Money*, 95.
52. Ibid., 96; Opitz, *Traditional Money*, 227; Quiggin, *Primitive Money*, 268; "Inside Indonesia, Sail Indonesia Rally: Alor, Aug. 7, 2007," http://www.sailariel.com/Rally/07Alor.htm (accessed Oct. 22, 2008).
53. Quiggin, *Primitive Money*, 207.
54. R. Mauny, "The Western Sudan," *African Iron Age*, 82.
55. Quiggin, *Primitive Money*, 51–52.
56. Opitz, *Traditional Money*, 344–350.
57. Quiggin, *Primitive Money*, 68–70; Einzig, *Primitive Money*, 162.
58. Quiggin, *Primitive Money*, 64–65, pl. 1, 12, pl. 3, 4; Ettore Calchera and Matteo Truddaiu, "Ferrimoneta dell'Africa Equatoriale," *Notiziario del Centro Numismatico Valdostano* Anno II No. 5 (ottobre/dicembre 2006), 12–13, http://www.cnvaldostano.it/Notiziario/Notiziario%20n.5_web.pdf (accessed Oct. 23, 2008).
59. Sophie Drakich, "African Marriage Money,"*Bank of Canada Review* Summer 2005, 2.
60. Scott Semans, "African Ethnographic Money: Weapon Monies. Liganda," http://www.coin coin.com/seXX2.htm (accessed Oct. 23, 2008); Francine Farr, "African Pre-Coin Money Metal

Sculpture: The John B. Henry Collection. Blades: #075–077," http://www.henrycollection.org/#Blades (accessed Oct. 23, 2008); Quiggin, *Primitive Money*, 64.

61. Robert D. Leonard Jr., "Kissi Kilindi Money," *The Centinel* 48:3 (Fall 2000), 15–20.
62. Quiggin, *Primitive Money*, 87, pl. 1, 10; Johansson, *Nigerian Currencies*, 36.
63. Sigler, *Strange Money* (1962), 16; Mosher, *Story of Money*, 51, 70; Francine Farr, "African Pre-Coin Money Metal Sculpture: The John B. Henry Collection. Hammers: #110," http://www.henrycollection.org/#Hammers.
64. Mosher, *Story of Money*, 28, 51, 77.
65. Ibid., 29–30; Mosher, "French Cameroons, Africa," *Coin Topics* 7 (June–Sept. 1937), 17.
66. Morris Siegel, "The Mackenzie Collection: A Study of West African Carved Gambling Chips," *Memoirs of the American Anthropological Association* 55 (1940), 15–16, 18–21, 26–28.
67. Quiggin, *Primitive Money*, 71–72; Mosher, *Story of Money*, 28–29.
68. Robert D. Leonard Jr., "The Stone Money of Yap," *The Centinel* 41:1 (Spring 1993): 31–34.
69. P.C. Ozanne, "Ghana," *The African Iron Age*, 36–65, but especially 40–41; Quiggin, *Primitive Money*, 60–61; Hans M.F. Schulman, *Public Coin Auction of the Howard D. Gibbs Collection, Part III* (New York: Jan. 26–27, 1971), 22, lots 286–287; Howland Wood, "Stone Money of Africa," *The Numismatist* 24:2 (Feb. 1911), 50.
70. Quiggin, *Primitive Money*, 61; Dr. H.J. Runge, "Kautschukkugeln, Steine und Tabak." *money-trend* Nov. 1987, 33–37.
71. Einzig, *Primitive Money*, 72–75; Banning and Pavlish, "Observations on Primitive Money," 2424–2426.
72. Quiggin, *Primitive Money*, 184–186, pl. 18; Opitz, *Traditional Money*, 236–237; *World Culture Encyclopedia*, "Rossel Island Economy," 2008, http://www.everyculture.com/Oceania/Rossel-Island-Economy.html (accessed Oct. 24, 2008).
73. Quiggin, *Primitive Money*, 149–151; Einzig, *Primitive Money*, 83.
74. Einzig, *Primitive Money*, 83–87.
75. Ibid., 87.
76. Quiggin, *Primitive Money*, 130–131.
77. H.H. Montgomery, *The Light of Melanesia. A Record of Thirty-Five Years' Mission Work in the South Seas* (London: Society for Promoting Christian Knowledge, 1896), 126.
78. Einzig, *Primitive Money*, 64.
79. Art-Pacific.com, "Art-Pacific: Guide to artifacts. Solomon Islands crafts," http://www.art-pacific.com/artifacts/nuguinea/solomons/craftart.htm (accessed Oct. 25, 2008); Melanesian Handicraft, "Shell and Feather Money of the Solomon Islands," http://www.melanesianhandicraft.com.sb/The_Shell_Money.htm (accessed Apr. 24, 2008).
80. W. Davenport, "Red-Feather Money," 94–104; Art-Pacific.com, "Art-Pacific: Guide to artifacts."
81. Quiggin, *Primitive Money*, 296, 299–300; Taxay, *Money of the American Indians*, 77–80.
82. Mosher, *Story of Money*, 30; Andrew Battell, *The Strange Adventures of Andrew Battell*, ed. E.G. Ravenstein (London: The Hakluyt Society, 1901), 9, footnote 2 (quoting Duarte Lopez), 58; Quiggin, *Primitive Money*, 80, footnote 1.
83. Quiggin, *Primitive Money*, 263, 264, 266.
84. Ibid., 119, 130–137, 147–148; Jean Tarisesei, "Today is not the same as yesterday, and tomorrow it will be different again: *Kastom* in Ambae, Vanuatu," *The Australian National University Development Studies Network Development Bulletin* 51 (2000), 46–48, http://devnet.anu.edu.au/GenderPacific/pdfs/10_gen_gov_tarisesei.pdf (accessed Oct. 25, 2008).
85. Einzig, *Primitive Money*, 41–43.
86. Ibid., 62.
87. Quiggin, *Primitive Money*, 130–131.
88. Ibid., 133, 162; Opitz, *Traditional Money*, 305.
89. Quiggin, *Primitive Money*, 14–15, 300–302.
90. R.A.G. Carson, *Coins of the World*, New York: Harper & Brothers, 1962, 5–6, 587, pl. 1; Robert W. Wallace, "KUKALIM, WALWET, and the Artemision Deposit: Problems in Early Anatolian Electrum Coinage," *Agoranomia: Studies in Money and Exchange Presented to John H. Kroll* (New York: The American Numismatic Society, 2006), 37–48; David R. Sear, *Greek Coins and their values*, vol. 2, *Asia and North Africa* (London: Seaby Publications, 1979), 317–324; Donald Tzvi Ariel, "The Invention and Dissemination of the Idea of Coinage," Chicago Coin Club *Chatter* 48:11 (Nov. 2002), n.p.
91. Carson, *Coins of the World*, pl. 1–60.
92. Qian Jiaju, *History of Chinese Currency*, 6; Richard G. Doty, *Money of the World* (New York: The Ridge Press, 1978), 53.

93. Carson, *Coins of the World*, 464, pl. 12, 46, 50, 53, 54, 57, 58, 60, 62, 63; Daniel Sedwick and Frank Sedwick, *The Practical Book of Cobs*, 4th ed. (Winter Park, FL: Daniel Frank Sedwick, 2007); Cribb, *Cowrie Shells to Credit Cards*, 38–39.

94. David R. Sear, *Greek Coins and their values*, vol. 1, *Europe* (London: Seaby Publications, 1978), 25.

95. G.F. Hill, *The Ancient Coinage of Southern Arabia* (Chicago: Argonaut Inc., 1969).

96. Philip Grierson, *Byzantine Coins* (London: Methuen & Co. Ltd, 1982).

97. William D. Craig, *Supplement to Germanic Coinages* (n.p., n.d.), 9.

98. William D. Craig, *Germanic Coinages* (n.p.: William D. Craig, 1954), 216; Craig, *Supplement*, 9; John F. Lhotka, *Introduction to Medieval Bractates [sic]* (New York: Sanford J. Durst Numismatic Publications, 1989), 5.

99. Howard D. Gibbs, *Odd and Curious Money of the World: A Complete Register*, 3rd ed. (New York: Hans M. F. Schulman, 1956), 23.

100. Lhotka, *Medieval Bractates.*

101. Carson, *Coins of the World*, 106–112; Rodolfo Ratto, *Collection Edward A. Sydenham, Aes Grave Italique Monnaies Consulaires* (Lugano: Rodolfo Ratto, 1927, reprint Attic Books. Ltd., New York, 1974), 5, pl. V; Crawford, *Roman Republic*, 39–60, 145.

102. W. Carew Hazlitt, *The Coinage of the European Continent: Supplement to the Coinage of the European Continent*, new ed. (Chicago: Ares Publishers Inc., 1984), 167; Robert Friedberg, rev. and ed. by Arthur L. and Ira S. Friedberg, *Gold Coins of the World*, 6th ed. (Clifton, New Jersey: The Coin and Currency Institute, Inc., 1992), 525.

103. Japanese Numismatic Dealers Association, *Catalog* (Japanese text), 1982.

104. Friedberg, *Gold Coins of the World*, 439.

105. Opitz, *Traditional Money*, 228–230.

106. Peter Seaby, *The Story of the English Coinage* (London: B.A. Seaby, Ltd., 1952), 23; Spink, *Coins of England and the United Kingdom*, 37th ed. (London: Spink: 2002), 119–151.

107. Hunter Dickinson Farish, *Journal and Letters of Philip Vickers Fithian*, (Charlottesville: The University Press of Virginia, 1957), 39–40; Mendel Peterson, "Cut Coin in the United States." *The Numismatist* 75:5 (May 1962), 582–585; Jacob L. Grimm, *Archaeological Investigation of Fort Ligonier, Annals of Carnegie Museum*, vol. 42 (Pittsburgh, PA., Carnegie Museum, 1970), 82, 97.

108. Alex G. Malloy, Irene Fraley Preston, and Arthur G. Seltman, ed. by Allen G. Berman, *Coins of the Crusader States*, 2nd. ed. (Fairfield, CT: Berman Publications, 2004) 65–69, 83–86.

109. Album, *Islamic Coins*, 32.

110. Stack's, *Public Auction Sale: Americana Colonial and Federal Coins, Medals and Currency featuring Coins from the H.M.S. Feversham and Le Chameau Shipwrecks* (New York: Jan. 12–13, 1999), 7, 179.

111. Ralph C. Gordon, *West Indies Countermarked Gold Coins* (n.p.: Erik Press, 1987).

112. C.J. Howgego, *Greek Imperial Countermarks: Studies in the Provincial Coinage of the Roman Empire* (London: Royal Numismatic Society, 1985); F.G. Duffield, *A Trial List of the Countermarked Modern Coins of the World*, repr. from *The Numismatist*, 1962; Gregory G. Brunk, *Merchant and Privately Countermarked Coins* (Rockford, IL: World Exonumia Press, 2003); many others.

113. Classical Numismatic Group, Inc., *Triton VII* (New York: Jan. 12, 2004), lot 1069.

114. Peter Seaby, comp., *Coins and Tokens of Ireland* (London: B.A. Seaby Ltd., 1970), 70–71; Brian J. Danforth, "St. Patrick Coinage," *The Colonial Newsletter* 42:3 (Dec. 2002): 2371–2402.

115. Worldwide Bi-Metallic Collectors Club, "A History of bi-metallic coins," http://www.wbcc -online.com/bi-metal_history.html (accessed Oct. 28, 2008).

116. W. Carew Hazlitt, *The Coinage of the European Continent*, new ed. (Chicago: Ares Publishers Inc., 1984), 119.

117. Kurt Jaeger, *Die Deutschen Münzen seit 1871* (Basel: Münzen und Medaillen AG, 1979), 653–657.

118. M.R. Broome, *The 1780 Restrike Talers of Maria Theresia* (Oxford: The British Association of Numismatic Societies, 1972); Peter Harrigan, "Tales of a Thaler," *Saudi Aramco World* 54: 1 (Jan.–Feb. 2003): 14–23.

119. Pradeau, *Numismatic History of Mexico*, 53–54; Eric P. Newman, "The Earliest Money Using the Dollar as a Unit of Value," in *Perspectives in Numismatics* (Chicago: Ares Publishers Inc., 1986), 131–138; Eric P. Newman, *The Early Paper Money of America*, 4th ed. (Iola, WI: Krause Publications, 1997); R.S. Yeoman (ed. by Kenneth Bressett), *A Guide Book of United States Coins*, 63rd ed. (Atlanta: Whitman Publishing, LLC, 2009), 10.

120. F.M. Rose, *Chopmarks* (Dallas: Numismatics International, 1987); John M. Willem, *The United States Trade Dollar: America's Only Unwanted, Unhonored Coin* (Racine, WI: Whitman Publishing Company, 1965).

Chapter 6

1. Qian Jiaju, *History of Chinese Currency*, 49.
2. Polo, *Travels*, 202–203.
3. Elgin Groseclose, *Money and Man* (New York: Frederick Ungar Publishing Co., 1961), 120, 213–214.
4. Williams, *Money: A History*, 179–180.
5. Walter M. Loeb, *Catalog of Paper Money Around the World* (Port Washington, N.Y.: Universal Publishing Co., 1961), 43; Tom Chao, "Tom Chao's Paper Money Gallery: Hungary Hyperinflation Banknotes," http://www.tomchao.com/hb14.html (accessed Oct. 28, 2008).
6. Newman, *Early Paper Money*.
7. Groseclose, *Money and Man*, 132–144.
8. Shepard Pond, "The Assignats," *Selections from* The Numismatist, *Modern Foreign Currency*, repr. from Jan. 1935 issue (Racine, WI: Whitman Publishing Co., 1961), 175–183.
9. Norman Angell, *The Story of Money* (Garden City: Garden City Publishing Company, Inc., 1929), 264–265, 332–342; Chao, "Paper Money Gallery."
10. Newman, *Early Paper Money*, 24–26; Neil Shafer, *Let's Collect Paper Money!* (Racine, WI: Whitman Publishing Company, Inc., 1976), 31–32; BPCouncil, "Anti-Counterfeiting Technologies: Learning from U.S. Dollar Bills," http://www.bpcouncil.com/apage/767.php (accessed Oct. 28, 2008).
11. William Henry Atherton, *Montreal, 1535–1914: Under the French Regime 1535–1760*, vol. I, (Montreal: The S.J. Clarke Publishing Company, 1914), 275–277; Col. Phares O. Sigler, "Canadian Card Money," *Selections from* The Numismatist, *Modern Foreign Currency*, repr. from Sept., 1956 issue (Racine, WI: Whitman Publishing Co., 1961), 9–19; J.E. Charlton, *1974 Standard Catalogue of Canadian Coins Tokens & Paper Money*, 22nd. ed. (Toronto: Charlton International Publishing, Inc., 1973), 113.
12. Newman, *Early Paper Money*, 157.
13. Opitz, *Traditional Money*, 258–260.
14. Randolph Zander, *The Alaskan Parchment Scrip of the Russian American Company 1816–1867* (Bellingham, WA: Russian Numismatic Society, 1996).
15. Eric Rosenthal, *From Barter to Barclays* (Johannesburg: Barclays Bank D.C.O., 1968), 38.
16. Qian Jiaju, *History of Chinese Currency*, 164–168.
17. Opitz, *Traditional Money*, 98–99, 111, 204, 307; Gibbs, *Complete Register*, 14, 30, 38.
18. Stane Štraus, "Polymer Bank Notes of the World," http://www.polymernotes.org/ (accessed Oct. 29, 2008).
19. Yeoman, *Guide Book*, 358–380.
20. Dr. Philip W. Whiteley, *The Lesher Story*, repr. from *The Numismatic Scrapbook Magazine*, n.d. (1958).
21. NORFED, "The Story of the Liberty Dollar," "Liberty Dollar FAQ," "The Treasury Concurs: It's Legitimate!" http://www.norfed.org/html/story.asp, /faq.asp, /legal.asp (accessed Mar. 10, 2004); Clifford Mishler, "July held non-show numismatic experiences," *Numismatic News*, Aug. 31, 2004, 26, 28; Gordon Fraser, "'Liberty Dollar' causes concern in the region," *Citizen Online* Sept. 6, 2005, http://www.libertydollar.org/news-stories/pdfs/1160871262.pdf (accessed Nov. 1, 2008); Eric von Klinger, "Officials charge student spending Liberty Dollars," *Coin World*, Mar. 27, 2006, 94; Paul Gilkes, "Private group modifies Liberty Dollar obverse," *Coin World*, Oct. 23, 2006, 5; David L. Ganz, "Liberty, Ron Paul 'dollars' seized in raid," *Numismatic News*, Dec. 11, 2007, 30, 32.
22. William Charlton, "Leather Currency," *British Numismatic Journal*, vol. III, 1906, 311–328.
23. "Austrian Krones Struck in Leather," *The Numismatist*, May 1921, 204.
24. "Using Leather Money for Shoe Soles," *The Numismatist*, Feb. 1920, 86.
25. Yu Yan Tang, *Qián Chóu* (Tokens, Chinese text) 1997?; English summary, "China Bamboo Money," by Scott Semans, loosely inserted; Sigler, "Strange Money," 6–7.
26. Helen Wang, "Local bronze tokens issued in Jiangsu, China, in the 1930s," *The Numismatic Chronicle*, Vol. 157 (1997), 168.
27. Howland Wood, "The Sou Marqué." *The American Journal of Numismatics*, 48 (1915), 129.
28. Stephen Mihm, *A Nation of Counterfeiters* (Cambridge, MA.: Harvard University Press, 2007), 1–8, 233, 412.
29. Einzig, *Primitive Money*, 214–215; S.D. Goitein, *A Mediterranean Society*, vol. I (Berkeley: University of California Press, 1999), 240–248.

30. Abbott Payson Usher, "The Origin of the Bill of Exchange," *The Journal of Political Economy* 22:6 (June, 1914), 566–576; Neil Sowards, ed., *The Handbook of Check Collecting* (Fort Wayne: Neil Sowards, 1975), 8.
31. "History of Traveler's Checks Featured in Smithsonian Exhibit," *Numismatic News*, Mar. 16, 1964, 9.
32. Sowards, *Check Collecting*.
33. Lynda Lesowski, "Abernethy's Rock Money Served Oregonians," *Coin World*, Jan. 4, 1978, 38; Dudley L. McClure, *Tales of the Golden Beavers* (Iola: Krause Publications, 1978), 30–34.
34. Jacques Labrot, *Une Histoire Economique et Popular du Moyen Age: Les jetons et les méreaux* (Paris: Editions Errance, 1989).
35. Robert D. Leonard Jr., "Collecting U.S. Tokens: Challenges and Rewards," *Perspectives in Numismatics* (Chicago: Ares Publishers Inc., 1986), 177–194.
36. H.A. Ramsden, *Siamese Porcelain and Other Tokens* (Yokohama: Jun Kobayagwa Co., 1911), 4–7; Opitz, *Traditional Money*, 262–264.
37. Thomas Hudson, *Guide Book of Wooden Money*, 6th ed. (Gardena: Payne Publishing Co., 1966).
38. Charles V. Kappen and Ralph A. Mitchell, *Depression Scrip of the United States, Period of the 1930s: States A thru I* (San Jose: The Globe Printing Co., 1961), 2, 22–24, 33–34, pl. 8, 12.
39. Angell, *Story of Money*, 46.
40. Kappen and Mitchell, *Depression Scrip*, 84, pl. 50.
41. Jonathan Croall, *LETS Act Locally* (London: Calouste Gulbenkian Foundation, 1997); ComplementaryCurrency.org, "Online Database of Complementary Currencies Worldwide," http://www.complementarycurrency.org/ccDatabase/les_public.html (accessed Oct. 30, 2008).
42. Paul Glover, "A History of Ithaca HOURs," http://ithacahours.com/archive/0001.html (accessed Oct. 29, 2008); Ithaca HOURS, "Ithaca HOURS Local Currency Ithaca NY," http://www.ithacahours.org/ (accessed Oct. 29, 2008).
43. The Federal Reserve Board, "Fedwire Funds Transfer System," http://www.federalreserve.gov/paymentsystems/coreprinciples/default.htm (accessed Oct. 29, 2008).
44. SWIFT, "SWIFT history," http://www.swift.com/index.cfm?item_id=1243 (accessed Oct. 29, 2008).
45. Seth Lubove, "On the Backs of the Poor," *Forbes* 174: 10 (Nov. 15, 2004), 156–160.
46. "Timeline: The ATM's history," NetWorld Alliance LLC, http://www.atm24.com/NewsSection/Industry%20News/Timeline%20-%20The%20ATM%20History.aspx (accessed Oct. 29, 2008).
47. Ibid.; Jack Weatherford, *The History of Money* (New York: Three Rivers Press, 1997), 225–227; MasterCard Worldwide, "Company Milestones." http://www.mastercard.com/us/company/en/ourcompany/company_milestones.html (accessed Oct. 29, 2008).
48. Johnny Acton and Sean O'Grady, "Money, money, money: The history of cash," *The Independent* Oct. 16, 2007, http://www.independent.co.uk/money/invest-save/money-money-money-the-history-of-cash-397015.html (accessed Oct. 29, 2008).
49. Answers.com, "Smart Card," http://www.answers.com/topic/chip-card (accessed Oct. 29, 2008).
50. e-gold®, "Better Money," http://www.e-gold.com/unsecure/qanda.html (accessed Oct. 29, 2008).
51. PayPal™, "About Us," https://www.paypal-media.com/aboutus.cfm (accessed Oct. 29, 2008).
52. Galbraith, *Money*, 18–19.
53. Weatherford, *History of Money*, 227–228.
54. Ibid., 181–187.

SELECTED BIBLIOGRAPHY

While there are many specialized works on the primitive money of particular geographic areas, relatively few attempt to cover the subject as a whole. Those selected for inclusion below are either comprehensive works in their own right (perhaps limited to a single continent, however), histories of money itself with extensive coverage of primitive money, or in-depth studies of specific currencies with wider implications. Emphasis has been placed on well-researched studies relying chiefly on primary sources. Collector pricing information was not a criterion, since only *An Ethnographic Study of Traditional Money* by Charles J. Opitz provides that (in an addendum).

Balmuth, Miriam S. "The Monetary Forerunners of Coinage in Phoenicia and Palestine." In *International Numismatic Convention, Jerusalem, 27–31 December 1963: The Patterns of Monetary Development in Phoenicia and Palestine in Antiquity. Proceedings*, edited by A. Kindler, pp. 25–32, Pl. I–VI. Tel-Aviv: Schocken Publishing House, 1967.

Balmuth Miriam S., ed. *Hacksilver to Coinage: New Insights into the Monetary History of the Near East and Greece*. Numismatic Studies No. 24. New York: The American Numismatic Society, 2001.

Blair, Allen M. *A World of Money from the Earliest Times: A Concise Non-Eurocentric History of the World's Native Currencies*, 2nd ed. Alexandria, MN: Northcountry Publishing Co., 1997.

Cribb, Joe. *Money—From Cowrie Shells to Credit Cards*. London: British Museum Publications, 1986.

Curtis, James W., Col. "Media of Exchange in Ancient Egypt." In *Selections from* The Numismatist, *Ancient and Medieval Coins* (reprinted from May 1951 issue), 153–162. Racine: Whitman Publishing Company, 1960.

Du Puy, William Atherton. "The Geography of Money." *National Geographic* 52: 6 (Dec. 1927).

Einzig, Paul. *Primitive Money in its Ethnological, Historical and Economic Aspects*. London: Eyre & Spottiswoode, 1948, reprinted 1951.

Gillilland, Cora Lee C. *The Stone Money of Yap: A Numismatic Survey*. Washington: Smithsonian Institution Press, 1975.

Guehler, Ulrich. "Further Studies of Old Thai Coins." *Journal of the Siam Society* 35: 2 (1944): 147–172 (reprinted in *Siamese Coins and Tokens*, 1977).

———. "Some Investigations on the Evolution of the Pre-Bangkok Coinage." *Journal of the Siam Society* 36: 1 (1946): 23–37 (reprinted in *Siamese Coins and Tokens*, 1977).

———. "Notes on Old Siamese Coins." *Journal of the Siam Society* 37: 1 (1948): 1–25 (reprinted in *Siamese Coins and Tokens*, 1977).

Herbert, Eugenia W. *Red Gold of Africa*. Madison: The University of Wisconsin Press, 1984.

Jiaju, Qian. *A History of Chinese Currency (16th Century BC–20th Century AD)*. Hong Kong: Xinhua (New China) Publishing House, N.C.N. Limited, and M.A.O. Management Group Ltd., 1983.

Johansson, Sven-Olof. *Nigerian Currencies: Manillas Cowries and Others*, 2nd ed. Norrköping: Author, 1967.

Le May, Reginald. *The Coinage of Siam*. Bangkok: The Siam Society, 1932, reprinted 1977.

Mitton, Charles L. *Ethnic Groups, Artifacts and Traditional Money of Africa Cross Reference Guide*. Denver: Author, 2005.

Mosher, Stuart. *The Story of Money as Told by the Knox Collection. Bulletin of the Buffalo Society of Natural Sciences* 17: 2, 1936. (Reprinted 1950 with different pagination.)

Opitz, Charles J. *An Ethnographic Study of Traditional Money*. Ocala: First Impressions Printing, Inc., 2000.

———. *Traditional Money on Yap & Palau*. Ocala: First Impressions Printing, Inc., 2004.

Quiggin, A. Hingston. *A Survey of Primitive Money: The Beginnings of Currency.* London: Methuen & Co., Ltd., 1978.

Ridgeway, William. *The Origin of Metallic Currency and Weight Standards.* Cambridge: The University Press, 1892.

Sigler, Col. Phares O. "Strange Money of the World." Reprinted from *The Numismatist*, 1962.

Taxay, Don. *Money of the American Indians and Other Primitive Currencies of the Americas.* Flushing: Nummus Press, 1970.

Terrien de Lacouperie, A. *Catalogue of Chinese Coins From the VIIth Cent. B.C., to A.D. 621, Including the Series in the British Museum.* London: Trustees of the British Museum, 1892.

Williams, Jonathan, ed., with Joe Cribb and Elizabeth Errington. *Money: A History.* New York: St. Martin's Press, 1997.

PHOTO CREDITS

Unless otherwise credited, all images in this book are taken from the odd and curious money collection of Charles J. Opitz.

Page	Name	Credit
3	Flint roughout	From the author's collection
4	Hopewell stone disks	"The Hopewell Mound Group of Ohio," by Warren K Moorehead, in *Anthropology*, vol. VI, no. 5 (Chicago: Field Museum of Natural History, 1922)
5	Anatolian obsidian	From the author's collection
5	Mexican obsidian	From the author's collection
6	Ancient precoinage silver	I. Sztulman and E. Kessell, Tel Miqne-Ekron Excavation Project
7	Viking silver hoard	© The Trustees of the British Museum. All rights reserved.
7	Ruble	Courtesy of Dmitry Markov
8	Sycee side view	Courtesy of the author
9	Cyprus ox-hide ingot	© The Trustees of the British Museum. All rights reserved.
10	Swedish 10-daler plate	The Royal Coin Cabinet, Stockholm, Sweden
11	Gold nuggets	Courtesy of Kenneth Bressett
11	Mansa Musa	Courtesy of the author
12	Prospector	Courtesy of the author
13	British iron currency bars	© The Trustees of the British Museum. All rights reserved.
13	Ancient Briton	*Everyday Life in the New Stone, Bronze, & Early Iron Ages*, 2nd ed., by Marjorie & C.H.B. Quennell (London: Batsford, 1931)
14	Ankole cattle	International Livestock Research Institute
16	Maize	Hugh Iltis, Dept. of Genetics, University of Wisconsin
16	Irish slave girl	*Everyday Life in the New Stone, Bronze, & Early Iron Ages*, 2nd ed., by Marjorie & C.H.B. Quennell (London: Batsford, 1931)
17	African slaves	Courtesy of the author
20	Aztec god	© Foundation for the Advancement of Mesoamerican Studies, Inc., www.famsi.org
26	Northwest Coast Indian trade gun (bottom of page)	Minnesota Historical Society
27	Musket ball	From the author's collection
27	Hand turned wooden bowl	Courtesy of Esther Gasser, Country Shop Antiques and Gifts, Winnetka, IL (Robert D. Leonard Jr. photograph)
29	Marten pelt	Moscow Hide and Fur, Moscow, Idaho / www.hideandfur.com
32	Aztec cotton mantles	http://en.wikipedia.org/wiki/Codex_Mendoza
32	Hudson's Bay Co. blanket	Courtesy of Mitchell Museum of the American Indian, Evanston, IL (Robert D. Leonard Jr. photograph)
34	Iraq bread market	Field Museum of Natural History, Chicago (thanks to Carl Wolf for obtaining image)
35	Olive oil press	Robert D. Leonard Jr. photograph
36	Salt Caravan	Courtesy of Marco Fulle, www.stromboli.net
37	Peppercorns	Courtesy of the author
39	Carga of cacao beans, Mendoza Codex	http://en.wikipedia.org/wiki/Codex_Mendoza
40	World War II-era Hershey bars	Whitman image archives
41	Kyrgyzstan gum	From the author's collection
43	Russian vodka	Courtesy of the author
43	Johnny Walker Red	Courtesy DIAGEO North America
45	Opium poppy	http://flickr.com/photos/superfantastic/68321333
46	Cocaine	http://www.justice.gov/dea/concern/cocaine.html
47	Civil War-era U.S. postage stamps	Whitman image archives

PHOTO CREDITS

Page	Name	Credit
51	Rawenock	Courtesy of Kenneth Bressett
56	Aggry bead	*Fustat Finds*, edited by Jere L. Bacharach, copyright © 2002 by the American University of Cairo Press
60	Gold ring money	© The Trustees of the British Museum. All rights reserved.
61	Navajo silver jewelry	Courtesy of Kenneth Bressett
65	Chinese Shang Dynasty cowries	From the author's collection
72	Shark vertebrae	From the author's collection
73	Ancient shell rings	From the author's collection
74	Celtic ring money (knobbed)	From the author's collection
74	Celtic ring money (plain)	Courtesy of Bill & Rita Rosenblum
74	Celtic ring money (group)	Courtesy of Bill & Rita Rosenblum
75	Benin plaque showing manillas	© The Trustees of the British Museum. All rights reserved.
77	Painting from the tomb of Benia	Courtesy of Dr. Theirry Benderitter / www.osirisnet.net
83	"Ant-nose" money	Courtesy of Kenneth Bressett
84	Tin animals	© The Trustees of the British Museum. All rights reserved. / Courtesy of Joe Cribb
94	Yap stone and Charles J. Opitz	Photograph courtesy of Charles J. Opitz
98	Woodpecker scalp	American Numismatic Society
99	Human skulls	*The Natives of Sarawak and British North Borneo*, by H. Ling-Roth, Vol. 2 (London: Truslove & Hanson, 1896)
101	Lydian electrum lump	*Collecting Ancient Greek Coins*, by Paul Rynearson (Atlanta: Whitman Publishing, 2009)
102	Coins of Croesus	*100 Greatest Ancient Coins*, by Harlan J. Beck (Atlanta: Whitman Publishing, 2008)
102	Chinese square-holed cash coin	From the author's collection
102	Square coin, India	*A Catalog of Modern World Coins, 1850–1964*, 14th ed., by R.S. Yeoman, rev. & ed. by Arthur L. Friedburg (Atlanta: Whitman Publishing, 2008)
102	Scalloped coin, Sudan	*A Catalog of Modern World Coins, 1850–1964*, 14th ed., by R.S. Yeoman, rev. & ed. by Arthur L. Friedburg (Atlanta: Whitman Publishing, 2008)
102	Dolphin coin, Olbia	*Collecting Ancient Greek Coins*, by Paul Rynearson (Atlanta: Whitman Publishing, 2009)
102	Himyarite silver coin	From the author's collection
102	Byzantine gold hyperpyron	From the author's collection
102	Holphennig	From the author's collection
103	Bracteate	American Numismatic Society
105	Cut halfpence and farthing	From the author's collection
105	Cut Crusader gold	From the author's collection
105	Plugged Spanish Umayyad dirham	American Numismatic Society
105	West Indies plugged gold coin	American Numismatic Society
105	Countermarked ancient and Saudi Arabian coins	From the author's collection
106	Aksum bronze coin with gold inlay	From the author's collection
106	St. Patrick's farthing	*A Guide Book of United States Coins 2010*, 63rd ed., by R.S. Yeoman, ed. by Kenneth Bressett (Atlanta: Whitman Publishing, 2009)
106	Saxony porcelain coin	From the author's collection
108	Stockholms Banco	The Royal Coin Cabinet, Stockholm, Sweden
109	5 Euro, Israeli 10 Lirot, Croatian 5 Dinara	Courtesy of Alexandra Troxell
109	Hong Kong 1-cent note	From the author's collection
109	Confederate $100 note	Courtesy of Hugh Shull
109	Zimbabwe $100 trillion note	Courtesy of Kenneth Bressett
110	Continental currency note	*America's Money, America's Story*, 2nd ed., by Richard Doty, (Atlanta: Whitman Publishing, 2008)

INDEX

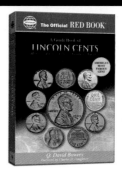
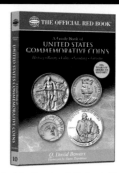